A-D/HD GUIDE

FOR DRIFTERS IN A SQUIRREL MOMENT

Testing, Diagnosis, and Treatment of A-D/HD

"The concept of **ADHD** as a disorder probably dates back to the late 18th century. Dr. Spero and Dr. Michael have written a comprehensive, up-to-date and useful guide for those of us who have to deal with ADHD now, either personally or professionally. I especially admired the discussion of the multiple etiologies that could give rise to the disorder, the assessment techniques, as well as treatment options; in addition, what rings throughout the work is respect and sympathy for those suffering from ADHD."

"This book has my enthusiastic recommendation."

Allan F. Mirsky, Ph.D., ABPP-CN
Adjunct Professor, Department of Psychiatry
Uniformed Services University
Bethesda, Maryland
June 11, 2019

Dr. Mitch Spero
Dr. Diann Dee Michael
Stable Life, L.L.C.
©2019

Copyright © 2025 by Mitchell Spero

All rights reserved. No part of this publication may be reproduced, distributed, or transmitted in any form or by any means, including photocopying, recording, or other electronic or mechanical methods, without the prior written permission of the copyright owner and the publisher, except in the case of brief quotations embodied in critical reviews and certain other noncommercial uses permitted by copyright law. For permission requests,write to the publisher, addressed "Attention: Permissions Coordinator," at the address below.

CITIOFBOOKS, INC.
3736 Eubank NE Suite A1
Albuquerque, NM 87111-3579
www.citiofbooks.com
Hotline: 1 (877) 389-2759
Fax: 1 (505) 930-7244

Ordering Information:
Quantity sales. Special discounts are available on quantity purchases by corporations, associations, and others. For details, contact the publisher at the address above.

Printed in the United States of America.

ISBN-13:   Softcover   979-8-89391-641-6
               eBook   979-8-89391-642-3

Library of Congress Control Number: 2025907017

Dedication

To the Late
Dr. Diann Dee Michael

Dr. Diann Dee Michael passed away prior to the publication of this book, and it is hoped that she will be remembered for her life time of work in the field of Psychology. For thirteen years, she worked with Dr. Mitch Spero, the owner of Stable Life, L.L.C. at Child & Family Psychologists.
Dr. Diann Dee Michael will be missed forever.
Dr. Mitch Spero then went on to establish Stable Life, L.L.C., his own corporation for his own publications of books and games, educational seminars, and more.

This book has an interesting history. Dr. Mitchell E. Spero and Dr. Diann Dee Michael presented a seminar at the 2002 Florida Psychological Association Annual Convention. The seminar was professionally videotaped, transcribed, and then edited into this current Publication. For comments and questions, consultation, and additional information the author of this book, Dr. Mitch can be reached at Stable Life, L.L.C.

Stable Life, L.L.C./ Dr. Mitch Spero
Telephone: 945-401-0126
Fax #: 954-587-7527
Local Tel: +1 505-444-6990
Fax #: +1 505-930-7244
info@citiofbooks.com
www.citiofbooks.com

We would like to acknowledge and thank these individuals for their editing, proofing, and typing of this book:

Allan F. Mirsky, Ph.D., ABPP-CN
Howard Marcus, Psy.D.
Joyce Warren
Marcia E. Dicks
Letitia Hoy
Tamara Waldorf

Forwards

Allan F. Mirsky, Ph.D., ABPP-CN
Marvin Lew, Ph.D., ABPP
Howard Marcus, Psy.D.
John Maurer, Ph.D.

By,
Allan F. Mirsky, Ph.D., ABPP-CN
Adjunct Professor, Department of Psychiatry
Uniformed Services University
Bethesda, Maryland
June 11, 2019

"The concept of ADHD as a disorder probably dates back to the late 18th century. Dr. Spero and Michael have written a comprehensive, up-to-date and useful guide for those of us who have to deal with ADHD now, either personally or professionally. I especially admired the discussion of the multiple etiologies that could give rise to the disorder, the assessment techniques, as well as treatment options; in addition, what rings throughout the work is respect and sympathy for those suffering from ADHD. This book has my enthusiastic recommendation.My research focus has always been on disorders of attention as well as the neuropsychological/cerebral underpinnings of normal and impaired attention. My research has concerned such entities as brain damage, epilepsy, schizophrenia, fetal alcohol syndrome, and other disorders, as well as ADHD."

Dr. Mirsky has been conducting research on normal and impaired attention since the 1950s. His earliest research efforts, under the guidance of Professor Dr. Haldor E. Rosvold, were supported by a V.A. grant to study effects of prefrontal lobotomy. This grant had been awarded to Professor Dr. John F. Fulton, whose work on chimpanzees with Dr. Carlyle Jacobsen showed possible beneficial effects on temperament of frontal lobe lesions.

Dr. Mirsky's subsequent research efforts were supported by a variety of sources, including the Foundations Fund for Research in Psychiatry, the National Science Foundation, and most of all by the National Institute of Mental Health (NIMH). In the early 1960s he and a colleague Professor Dr. Conan Kornetsky, were awarded a $1,000,000 Grant from NIMH (National Institute of Mental Health). During his career, most of his support, both as an intramural researcher, and as a Research Scientist awardee at Boston University, came from NIMH. His work has been honored by the International Neuropsychological Society, the American Board of Professional Psychology, the Maryland Psychological Association, and the City College of New York. Dr. Mirsky personally edited the Chapter on his theoretical Model of A-D/HD. Dr. Spero has the utmost respect for Dr. Mirsky, and is grateful for his help and support.

By,
Marvin Lew, Ph.D., ABBP
Licensed Psychologist/FL #PY6957, MA #PY3089

"Dr. Spero has a wealth of clinical wisdom and advice to share with others in this book. His experience dealing with a wide range of attention related problems will help others to better understand their own experience and that of their loved ones."

By,
John Maurer, Ph.D.
Licensed Psychologist/FL# PY3444

"This book provides the reader with an insightful understanding of A-D/HD. It is easy to read and digest. It provides insightful information in order to make an effective diagnosis of A-D/HD."

"To Child & Family Psychologists-my best wishes in your work. I appreciate Mitch's attendance and questions at this workshop. C. Keith Conners, Ph.D." November 10, 1993

Workshop Course Manual Attention-Deficit / Hyperactivity Disorder: Assessment and Treatment for Children and Adolescents Featuring C. Keith Conners, Ph.D. sponsored by Multi-Health Systems, Inc.

"To Mitch - Best Wishes" C. Keith Conners, Ph.D. June 22 & 23, 1996

Attention-Deficit / Hyperactivity Disorder: Assessment and Treatment for Children and Adolescents presented by C. Keith Conners, Ph.D. professor of Medical Psychology Duke University Medical Center. An Introductory Workshop Under the Auspices of Multi Health Systems, Inc.

"Attention-Deficit / Hyperactivity Disorder:
For Drifters in a Squirrel Moment
A Guide to Testing, Diagnosis and Treatment of A-D/HD
By Dr. Mitch Spero

© Copyright 2020

A-D/HD seems to be the defining disorder of the transition from the 20th to the 21st century. Whenever our children have trouble focusing, achieving, and completing tasks at home or at school, the question arises "Do they have an attention deficit?" While there are instances of inattention and over-activity in other cultures, it seems to be a particularly American phenomenon. Is there a cultural component; a dietary component; an environmental trigger? Are our children missing some important component in early childhood as mothers return to work during their infancy and turn them over to group care? Are there alternatives to psycho-stimulants and external monitoring that amounts to external behavioral control of the child's early development? Even with positive benefits of the psycho-stimulants, what is wrong with their brains that they are not working in synchrony with other children? Are our expectations too high of children that we want to homogenize them and create a "normal" construct out of individuals?

There are many, many books on Attention-Deficit/ Hyperactivity Disorder. Some are scholarly and focus entirely on professional research. While being important for researchers and scholars, these books do little to help the family, teacher, or physician struggling to aid and understand a child whose best intentions still do not enable them to complete three tasks in a row consistently. Other books are self-help books, often packed with great advice, but usually not well substantiated as to the procedures suggested, and more problematic, often very partisan and narrow in focus. Other books are presented by professionals who have a particular approach to promote, a result of their practice or their research, often excellent in nature, but again, narrow in focus.

This book intends to contribute to the public and the literature in a unique manner. While written in easy to read, straightforward language that can be grasped and understood by everyone, it will be based on a thorough review of much of the current literature.

Popular approaches and treatments will be included, as will erudite, scholarly research, and innovative, promising, but unresearched approaches. References will be available for everyone to further delve into interesting aspects for themselves.

In providing an accessible and straightforward written presentation of what is known at the time of this publication, paired with exhaustive, scholarly research, we think that this book can create a more informed consumer, educator, and practitioner, as well as stimulate thought from a firm knowledge base, upon which to launch a more cooperative collaboration in finding more effective psychological testing and treatments for the future.

Many individuals of all ages with Attention-Deficit/Hyperactivity Disorder say that they often feel as though their attention **drifts**. This book is written to help the Drifters in a Squirrel Moment. Thank you for buying, reading, and sharing this book with others.

Authors:
Dr. Mitch Spero and Dr. Diann Dee Michael
Licensed Psychologists and Authors in the State of Florida, U.S.A

ABOUT THE AUTHOR

Dr. Mitch Spero is the President/Owner of Stable Life, L.L.C. His publishing company CITIOFBOOKS, INC. publishes and internationally distributes books and games for children and adolescents. Dr. Mitch Spero is also the Author of the Book and Game, "Florida The Turtle Who Thinks He's a Dog Finds His Feelings." This previously published book and game helps children and adolescents to overcome Anxiety, Fears and Shyness, and to understand and share their feelings! This A-D/HD Book and Game by Dr. Mitch Spero incorporates Psychological Evaluation, Differential Diagnosis, the Possible Etiologies and Theoretical Frameworks, and Treatment of A-D/HD.

Dr. Mitch Spero, who for years expected to become a Veterinarian, shifted his interest to the Psychological Study of Animal Behavior, and then specifically to Clinical Psychology, the Science of Human Behavior. A-D/HD Evaluation and Treatment is one of Dr. Mitch Spero's Career Area of Specialization. As a Licensed Psychologist and Director of Child and Family Psychologists, in Sunrise, FL and the Owner of Stable Life, L.L.C., Dr. Spero, for decades has developed and maintained a steady flow of Psychological Evaluations, second opinions, and Psychological Treatment of children, adolescents, and adults who have been diagnosed as A-D/HD. Dr. Mitch Spero has been selected as an Honored Member of "Trademark Top Doctors of America Honors Edition 2019," which indicates, "For HE HAD A DREAM SET OUT TO ACHIEVE IT AND SUCCEEDED." Dr. Spero was also honored as the "2018 and 2019 TOP LICENSED PSYCHOLOGIST IN FLORIDA" by PATIENT REVIEWS CERTIFIED TOP DOCTOR" and was featured in "Top Doctors' Magazine THE TOP DOCTORS IN PEDIATRICS, DENTISTRY, ONCOLOGY, PLASTIC SURGERY, ORTHOPEDIC SURGERY AND MORE." He is also internationally known as having served as the Pro-Bono Psychological Evaluator of Elian Gonzalez. He has benefitted by attending seminars and personally interacting with many of the most knowledgeable Psychologists, who have studied and published works about ADHD. This book was written to educate and help all of you who cope with ADHD.

In 2006, Mitchell E. Spero,Psy.D. was the recipient of the FPA "Distinguished Psychologist Award For Significant Ongoing Contributions to The Florida Psychological Association Advancing The Mission of FPA and to the Profession of Psychology as a member of FPA." Dr. Mitch Spero has been known as the Doctor of Psychology, a live international speaker, and an author of Books and Games. Dr. Spero lives in Florida. He is a Third Degree Black Belt in Tae-Kwon-Do, enjoys playing the guitar, caring for animals, kayaking, camping, horseback riding, the beach, public speaking and spending time with his family and friends.

TABLE OF CONTENTS

CHAPTER 1

What is A-D/HD?

We hear all the time, "Mrs. Jones, Johnny just cannot sit still in the reading circle, I think your child might be hyperactive." Family visits are often grueling, and we find relatives asking, "Dear, have you ever thought of getting some medicine for that boy? He is all over the place." Parents regularly receive similar statements in school reports, "Johnny would do much better if he paid attention." Trying to help their child, parents find every teacher's conference starting with, "Jane just cannot sit still, she is playing with papers and doing everything but listening to the lesson."

These comments and the difficulties bring you to the questions: Is it possible that your child has an attention disorder? Is he or she hyperactive? How do you know and understand why they are the way they are?

In discussing the issue with others, we also hear, "John's just a boy, that's all. He does not like to be in one place all the time." Friends and relatives add, "Jane's bored in school maybe she's just smarter than the other kids." Very often one parent then comes to the realization, "Well I was just like that in school too, and I turned out alright." Next, there is the fear of consequences often spoken in media reports, "No one's going to put my kid on pills and turn him into a zombie." Finally, there is the inevitable theory that if it is just a stage of childhood, "Leave it alone, she will grow out of it", or the ill-informed conclusion that "he's just not trying," or, "I know John's not paying attention, he is just lazy."

These are the kinds of statements the parents of children with attention disorders and/or hyperactivity hear all of the time. What is the "normal" level of activity or interest? Don't all children get bored and fidget? Who can sit still for that boring seatwork all the time, anyway? How do you determine if a child has A-D/HD, and what is the actual diagnosis anyhow?

No diagnosis of childhood disorders generates more theories or controversy than A-D/HD. Historically seen first as a neurological disorder primarily caused by prenatal oxygen deprivation or birth respiratory trauma, then primarily as a failure in adequate parenting, the diagnosis of A-D/HD has come a long way in the last 4 decades and yet it remains controversial and charged with theoretical rivalries, public and professional debate, and masked confusion among both practitioners and the general public.

Somewhere, lost in the furor, is a small child whose parents are perplexed and distressed, whose teachers are frustrated and annoyed, and whose sense of self is one of anguish and self-hatred; the A-D/HD child expresses stress, failure, and disappointment. Surrounded by the confusion of anger of those who are supposed to raise, teach, and treat them, they find themselves often alone and misunderstood. Consequently, they find themselves feeling rejected, blamed and most sadly of all, punishing themselves for the failures of the adults around them to correctly identify and aid them in their growth and development.

Our book has been written to aid parents, teachers, children, and other adults interested in understanding and helping children, adolescents, and adults with attention disorders with and without hyperactivity. A-D/HD is a condition that has plagued eager and excited learners for centuries. However, it is one of the most misunderstood, mistreated, and misdiagnosed disorders of childhood and adolescence.

Creating havoc with self-esteem and a concept of self-acceptance, A-D/HD strikes at the very foundation of the child's development, his or her early school years, and early socialization experiences. These first few experiences in a child's life can create the template for a lifelong pattern of self-doubt and self-recrimination. This book intends to clear the smoke and aid in the understanding and improvement of the life of those children, adolescents, and adults who read it.

Diagnosis

One of the difficulties with regard to the current term A-D/HD is that the diagnosis, which is defined by the and the DSM-5, Diagnostic Statistical Manual-5, of the American Psychiatric Association and the I.C.D.-10, is based on behavioral criteria rather that upon any causative factors of etiological background. Diagnostically, there is no distinction made regarding etiology, a term specifying why and how the disorder has developed. However, the causative factors do make a difference in how psychologists plan and implement treatment. There is a lot of confusion in the field with regard to the multiple theoretical perspectives of many professionals with many different points of view. Diagnosis based on the behavioral symptoms alone of A-D/HD is not adequate to develop the best and most efficient treatment plan, especially if there is no specified etiology.

Neurological, Behavioral, and Genetic Factors

There are multiple routes by which a child can arrive at the diagnosis of A-D/HD. There is a large majority of the A-D/HD population that has a neurological impairment that interferes with the incoming processing of information, its storage, or the output of action based upon information. On the other hand, there is a large percentage of children as well as adults who have been identified as A-D/HD, who in fact have a behavioral disorder with no form of any neurological impairment. As a behavioral disorder, learning and reinforcement of behaviors sometimes leads to inconsistency in attending and processing information, and an unpredictability of output.

Data does indicate that A-D/HD tends to run in families and there is increasing information that there is a genetic factor, and possibly an identifiable gene that affects the sustaining of attention. This data suggests that A-D/HD is similar to forms of epilepsy in that the brain has short lapses that affect attention, and that there is a hereditary factor with regard to these lapses.

Bored, Lazy or Just Doesn't Pay Attention

The treatment planning and implementation really must take into account the etiology for proper treatment to proceed effectively and expeditiously. Identifying the cause of an individual's attention deficit would also remove the stigma of responsibility from the child, adolescent, or adult entirely, thus challenging the notions of, "He's just bored" or "She's just lazy", which demoralizes a person's self-esteem and feelings of acceptance. Actually, even if the individual's attention problems result from inconsistent early learning, the person can hardly be blamed for the subsequent resulting behavior. Destigmatizing A-D/HD would advance the field, increase understanding, and aid children, adolescents, and adults in their authentic struggle with a condition not of their will or making.

Hidden Criticism about A-D/HD

Other moral critique hides in attitudes based on superstitions rather than facts. Only a century ago we witnessed people diagnosed with schizophrenia pass from the torturous punishments of hot and cold baths and flogging, to more humane understanding, effective empirically based treatment. This century's task is to repeat the process of knowledge, acceptance, and understanding leading to proper evaluation and treatment of A-D/HD. To bring about the disbursement of knowledge. It is time for practitioners, parents, teachers, and the individuals themselves to lose or replace notions such as, "He just needs to pay attention and just try harder," to an honest recognition that A-D/HD individuals suffer from a disruption of attention and/or of impulsivity and hyperactivity which is not of their own wish or making.

CHAPTER 2

The Processes That Make Up A-D/HD

Executive Function:
"I'll pay attention, plan and execute the instructions, Sir!" vs.
"What did you just say to me?"

Within the realm of neurological impairment there are two specific types of cognitive dysfunction. One focuses primarily on the **Executive Functioning.** Executive function usually refers to the frontal part of the brain and thus this theory focuses on frontal lobe integrity in individuals with A-D/HD. Executive functioning refers to the decision making meaningfulness and processing of information, task completion, and demonstrating appropriate behaviors. Practitioners with this theoretical emphasis lead the country in directing treatment and research.

Vigilance:
"Oh boy, this is important!" vs "Huh?"

However, there are also other practitioners that look at vigilance, or attention, as a kind of lower level function that involves a completely different set of brain structures. This approach focuses upon structures in the brain stem, such as the Reticular Activating System, as being essential in the recognition of important information and also in the sustaining of attention until all relevant information has been gathered.

Distractibility:
"This is interesting, now what was I doing?" vs. "Where was I?"

Often people describe an A-D/HD individual as being very "distractible." For many years most practitioners talked about A-D/HD as being primarily an increased form of distractibility which is certainly the way many parents and even adult A-D/HD patients experience their own attention deficit. Parents have observed their children's behavior and state, and often said, "They get distracted." However, the current base of research does not support distractibility as a primary function in A-D/HD. Many children who suffer from Attention Deficit Disorder are not more distractible than the average child of their age. All children get distracted. Distractibility is also a function of the average non-clinical population of children as well as the A-D/HD population. Children in general can differ and lose focus of the task at hand.

The difference is that A-D/HD children **cannot return to the original relevant stimuli after the distraction.** This is a very important distinction, because in the process of becoming distracted which is quite a normal function for children, A-D/HD children cannot return to the place from which they **drifted.** For the A-D/HD individual this presents quite a serious problem because an individual with average neurological functioning is able to return to the specific point of distraction. The A-D/HD individual simply cannot do that. Instead, they will most likely **continue to drift to the next stream of awareness or consciousness**, thus shifting farther and farther from the starting point. The A-D/HD child, adolescent, or adult is then hard pressed to recall where they began **drifting**, and the usual experience is one of, " I don't remember" when asked why they did not finish the task which they began?

Sustaining vs. Selective Attention

Sustaining Attention:
"Keep paying attention, keep paying attention,
keep paying attention!"

Difficulty sustaining attention over a long period of time has been documented as specifically being one of the main problem areas for A-D/HD individuals who experience inattention without Hyperactivity and/or Impulsivity problems, in that they cannot attend, maintain, and sustain attention. Tests that measure their ability to focus and sustain attention have continuously corroborated this as an identifiable and measurable primary deficit in these individuals' level of cognitive functioning.

Selective Attention:
"There's so much happening,
what is the most important thing to pay attention to?"

The next issue is that of selective attention. We are usually experiencing two or three stimuli. For example, you may simultaneously have an itch on your foot and hear a noise in the hallway and have a need to stretch your legs. Thus, you always have more than one stimulus competing for your attention. The A-D/HD child often has a problem in selecting the appropriate stimuli upon which to focus. In Dr. Michael's research she notes that this problem area in particular, affects the A-D/HD child with mixed impulsivity and inattention, rather than the ADD child who experiences inattention without impulsivity.

Input or Output Disorder

Another theoretical issue is that A-D/HD is viewed as either an input disorder, which is a problem of filtering incoming perceptions, or an output disorder, which is a problem of inhibiting behaviors. Generally, attention deficit with hyperactive behavior is conceived as a disinhibitory processing problem, (Russell Barkley, M.D., 1994), meaning that these children's behavior lacks restraint, therefore is unacceptable.

A Current Question in The Research

Major theorists in the field line up on one side or the other on the issue, but it appears that A-D/HD individuals have both a filtering problem and an output problem. It is possible for clinicians to differentiate these two important factors with extensive neuropsychological batteries, but most parents and insurance companies will not expend the funds necessary for such extensive, psychological evaluations. Some A-D/HD patients have more of a filtering problem than a disinhibitory problem, and vis versa; and there are some people who experience both of these types of problems. Hence, it seems that without extensive psychological and neuropsychological data, it is prudent to proceed as if the problem is not either, but is instead both.

Memory Issues in A-D/HD

Learning Efficiency:
"I did study, but I just can't remember it!"

Another separate issue is that of learning efficiency. People who have attention disorders, particularly children [because adults and even teenagers tend to learn to compensate quite well over their years of trial and error] have great difficulty learning because they are under-responsive to reinforcement. Children with attention disorders often do not respond to reinforcement with the same magnitude of behavioral change; nor do they consider most reinforcements to be as consistent or important.

Mental Health Professionals in private practice know that parents will come into our offices and say that they have tried everything, and somehow many different approaches worked for a little while, but then stopped working. This phenomenon is a characteristic of A-D/HD children, and it is helpful for parents to understand that although there will be a diagnosis made, it is possible that an A-D/HD child may be resistant to the strength or the type of reinforcer, and although it may have worked for three other children, it may not work with this particular child. This often relieves parents of their own guilt and frustration. Suddenly, these parents say, "Maybe it's not my fault after all, I'm not doing this wrong, this really is a functional characteristic of my child." This can be a very beneficial parental insight.

When the A-D/HD child does learn, they tend to generalize their learning to other situations less complete than the typical child, regardless of their level of intelligence. This concept may be somewhat confusing particularly with intellectually gifted A-D/HD individuals. It is frustrating even for psychologists who have taught A-D/HD patients in various methods of cognitive behavioral training techniques, because the parents are not able to generalize very effectively from the clinical training setting to the myriad of situations in the real world. In our practice we emphasize the process of utilizing each cue towards generalization to facilitate the process of learning with ease.

Impulsive Behavior

Another important characteristic of A-D/HD children is their impulse control problem, such as blurting out commands, hitting a younger brother or sister, not staying seated when expected to do so. Those behaviors are commonly observed as primary symptoms which often concern parents and teachers. It is as if the delay of gratification is impossible, and they simply can't wait to get on to do what they want to do instead of the task at hand. This pattern of behavior can cause frustration on the part of parents with their child's insistent and demanding style of behavior. This characteristic can lead to a frustrating interpersonal communication style of functioning, and it can often lead to a disruptive, agitating, and negative experience on part of parents, siblings, teachers, and peers.

Figuring Out What's Important and Setting Priorities

The focusing of attention is an executive level of cognitive functioning, because it involves interpreting social meaning or what is the most important information of which to focus upon. Social meaning has to be a much more complex higher level of function than the reticular activating function for example. So, being clearly differentiated and classified in its approach to a theoretical understanding of the disorder, we want to at least recommend the consideration of The Luria Model in the process of assessment and diagnosis of A-D/HD.

The Combination of Attention-Deficit/Hyperactivity Disorder and Learning Disabilities

In 30-70% of the cases of A-D/HD there is some form of an underlying learning disability. However, the research has reported many different concordances. To understand learning disabilities, it is important to assess the neurological pathways. This approach is extremely helpful when working with schools in regard to receptive disabilities. For example, a child may not be able to receive and encode information. This is concomitant to sensory input, but also involves the vigilance factor and productive disabilities. The areas in question may be: can the child demonstrate what he or she has learned, and is he or she able to then reproduce the information? Very often, children who are doing poorly in school and are having difficulty with spelling and math, but not so much in reading, may have a production disability. More simply put, they are able to complete the task at hand, but they just cannot do it on demand. For example, they cannot complete the task within the time requirements which the teacher imposes; they need a longer span of time and more cueing in order to be able to produce what they have already learned. We have often helped these individuals by conducting Psychological Evaluations to have them officially granted the special accommodation of extended test taking time on State or Nationally Standardized Tests.

The next area is what we call consolidation disabilities. There are some children who can take in information quite well, they can produce it, but they feel like a sieve, in that the new information does not seem to stay; it seems to fall through the floor. In consolidation difficulties, children learn, and they can even store information into short or medium range long-term memory, but they cannot use it again a week later. For example, a child who is gifted, but who cannot distinguish between beef, pork, and chicken has a categorization problem. The gifted child may be a mature child who knows many categories, but is not consolidating the information properly. For consolidation, as psychologists, we utilize repetition requirements, which are then modified to employ many types of different cues.

Also, motivational factors interact in A-D/HD to a great extent, because a child who is not interested, loses focus very quickly. If the subject matter is something that they are intrinsically interested in, because there is immediate feedback, i.e. a video game or music; they can stay focused continuously. Yet, it is the lack of motivation that can make it so difficult for these children to learn a ten word spelling list. The learning of a spelling list, simply is not intrinsically motivating. However, this is often a presentation problem on the part of many educational systems. Nonetheless, trying to augment the bland presentation of important information into something that sustains an A-D/HD child's attention requires a lot of technical expertise.

These types of children really need a kind of multi-modal approach to learning, since hearing the information in a dry presentation, even though they are very bright, just does not consolidate the information for them. Educational Consultations of a Team Approach can address these specific accommodations.

CHAPTER 3

Theoretical Models:
Aleksandr Romanovich Luria. Ph.D.

The Luria model is not as widely known as it should be in the United States. Researchers had a different theoretical approach to neurological function, and language translations slowed down distribution just as with Swiss Psychologist Jean Piaget's theories in the 1940's and 50's, which only became popularized in the 60's and 70's. on the other hand, the distribution of Luria's Theory has increased since the popularity of neuropsychological doctoral level coursework as an addition to general clinical psychology training.

The Luria Model

The Luria Model looks at the brain function in terms of three different systems. The first area is the **Arousal System**, which is controlled by the **Reticular Activating System** located in the lower brain and brainstem/nervous system, and functions as the "alert system". It is the part of the brain that awakens us when we start to fall asleep while driving. There is a loop from the Reticular Activating System to the frontal lobe that maintains vigilance and attention because of a higher level meaningfulness of the input and the task. That loop functions very rapidly, and does not involve conscious, higher level cognitive functioning. Unfortunately, in many A-D/HD children, the arousal system is not quite adequate in one or more parts of the loop. The sensory input, the processing, the consolidation, or the meaningfulness factors can be slower to engage and coordinate than the necessary timing for acquiring the information and responding to it in a sustained fashion. Paying attention is more difficult for them. Instead, they **drift**.

The second area is the **Sensory System**, which receives input from our visual sense, auditory sense, and tactile feedback. These are the three most important aspects of neurological feedback for information detection and learning, especially in an academic setting. Sometimes kinesthetic feedback is important in the pursuit of success in sports. Fine motor feedback is very complex and intimately involved in the writing phase of learning which stores input as one writes and produces output simultaneously. There are many children who are not good visual, auditory, or kinesthetic processors, and testing can identify these deficits. They often have a different presentation than the children who primarily have a deficit only in the reticular activating system.

The Reticular Activating System is considered to be more global in establishing overall vigilance. The **Sensory System** is more specific, but both systems are engaged in the learning process, and both deeply affect school performance, and the actual experience of school for the child.

Another aspect to the Sensory System is known as **Cross Modal Integration**. Right now, as you read this you may also be listening to your surroundings, and you may even be taking notes. All three functions are somehow coordinated. Many attention deficit individuals cannot coordinate two things, much less three. However, at this point and time we are unaware of the development of any specific tests that aid us in breaking the Sensory System down into separate components. In the future, the field of psychology may have assessment techniques for measuring the Sensory System, and even the specific type of breakdown of sensory processing which occurs.

The third function, according to the Luria Model, is known as the **Output and Planning System**. It is the executive function. It is a frontal lobe function, and our level of motor output is one of these types of functioning. Parents will come and tell us as psychologists, that their children seem to pay attention, and yet they cannot hit a ball. A lot of times, small and gross motor functions have been observed by parents to be deficient in A-D/HD children from very early on in life. We suggest that clinicians note that information, and then start to conjecture and create a hypothesis that there may be some problem in motor strip executive function, and also even in speech production.

Often for A-D/HD individuals, there is a lag in the time prior to their verbal response or answer to a question. Very often they do extremely well with almost everything, until they have to perform verbally. Then, when they perform orally they may even experience themselves as being slow. They may complain, because in the other areas of their functioning, they may be within the normal range or even considerably advanced. However, with regard to speech production, there might be a hesitancy, which is not stuttering, but actually an executive dysfunction in terms of speech production. Speech production uses a different area of the brain, and that hesitation can be ameliorated if we identify that processing as being the primary problem. Delays are also often found in decision making processes, and deficits in this area are even more global in their effect on overall cognitive performance.

Different parts of the brain are related to each of these various types of function.   There are children who have mild to moderate or even severe deficits, in the sensory system, executive function, and in reticular activating system. However, there are some children, adolescents, and also adults, who have only one area that is considered to be dysfunctional. Hence, there are some individuals who have more global deficits, and others who have very specific deficits.

A complete Diagnostic Interview assists mental health professionals in our treatment planning. For example, if someone does not have a global dysfunction, we are not helping them by spending hours and hours in psychotherapy focusing on an area in which they do not need help. If they do not have an executive dysfunction, there is really no point in doing a lot of higher level problem solving and decision making. It is not an ineffective therapeutic approach to provide work in this area, but it is not necessary in terms of what we are actually trying to ameliorate with a person with intact executive functioning abilities.

In terms of the application of this theory, Luria talks about one of proximal development; where he is actually asking us to gauge the extent to which the child can learn on their own, as compared to what they are able to learn with assistance. The boundary between what the child can learn on their own vs. the requirement of help is the zone of proximal development that requires educational guidance and support. Luria's model is more similar to the words of a coach or guide, rather than a dominating teaching style. Luria actually believes as Piaget did, that the children will learn on their own if they are not impeded, that they have a natural curiosity, that they have a zest for knowledge, and that they will seek out new information unless there are some internal or external barriers. Therefore, Luria suggests that looking at the zone of proximal development is helpful in understanding and aiding A-D/HD individuals in their cognitive development, and in their learning of skills they need to return to self-instruction.

Luria also talks about internal verbalization of a script in the cognitive-behavioral vernacular, that everybody has for every activity. We all have scripts of which we are not always immediately aware of cognitively. In particular, A-D/HD children in fact, often do not have these types of scripts. They have not been able to effectively internalize instructions, and they do not do it naturally. For these individuals, this process must be learned.

DONALD MICHENBAUM, Ph.D.

Critique of The Luria Model

Donald Michenbaum, Ph.D., who is not a neuropsychologist, critiqued the Luria Model from a different perspective. He identified self-instructed training as being helpful in inhibiting aggressive or impulsive activity in children. Also, in addition to needing direct training for verbal cues, sequential verbal cues are also considered to be necessary. Hence, one verbal cue is often not enough. When you give three instructions to an A-D/HD child, they may do the first two and then turn and say, "I know you gave another instruction, but that was too much." Therefore, the sequencing of their instruction needs to be much more deliberate than that which is directed to a child or adult who is not A-D/HD.

CHAPTER 4

PSYCHOLOGICAL EVALUATION PROCESS OF THE ATTENTION-DEFICIT/HYPERACTIVITY DISORDER

The use of continuous performance tests (C.P.T.) in the Psychological Evaluation of A-D/HD individuals must be addressed. It is believed that less than one third of the psychologists in the U.S. use this type of assessment technique. We strongly recommend C.P.T. assessment measures, because there is no one test that can in and of itself completely measure and support the diagnosis of A-D/HD. C.P.T.s also add computer generated data that assesses inattention and aspects of hyperactivity, such as inhibition of impulsiveness.

The Continuous Performances Tests began in the 1940's with Haldor Rosvold of the Royal Canadian Army in WWII. In assessing the effects of brain injury in wounded soldiers he noted what he referred to as "microsleeps" and breaks in concentration. This type of a break in consciousness occurs when you are talking to someone, and then in the blink of an eye, they seem to **drift**, and then they are immediately attentive once again. Those of us in psychology tend to do that constantly. We are present, but are thinking in terms of theoretically based treatment intervention, and then we rapidly return our focus to our patients and implement the intervention in the psychotherapy session. A-D/HD individuals often can't shift gears in the proper sequence. A-D/HD individuals have trouble getting back to the same exact spot where they were prior to losing focus. Yet that specific skill is so important interpersonally and vocationally later in life. This disconnection and reconnection at the wrong point in a conversation can be very frustrating, confusing, and difficult to follow as the listener. It can negatively affect the individual socially and occupationally.

In 1994, Russell Barkley, M.D. spoke in Broward County, Florida, and said that the disorder of which we are speaking of in the DSM-V would soon, no longer be called A-D/HD, but instead that the terminology would be a "Disinhibitory Disorder". C. Keith Conners', Ph.D. has described A-D/HD as a type of processing problem, while Mirsky said A-D/HD is similar to epilepsy. Each of these views may be correct in their different theoretical orientations. In A-D/HD there is often an inhibitory processing problem of the individual having **difficulty withholding a motor or verbal response**, and a tendency of jumping ahead. **"Disinhibitory Disorder" is then considered to be an inhibitory processing problem**. The point of interest, is that this is one specific measure that we are able to accurately assess and quantify with the use of Continuous Performance Tests.

Mirsky, speaks of many different Continuous Performance Tests. For example, one type of C.P.T. requires that the subject look at a computer screen, and then to respond only when the letter X flashes, and then only if the letter X is followed by the letter A.   Essentially, one is staring at the computer screen and being evaluated in the areas of the ability to sustained and focus attention, recovery or how they respond after making an error, and their variability of response times from the beginning to end of the test. These tests are inherently somewhat boring and frustrating but they are accurate in their evaluation of response times to one thousandth of a second. At the end of each testing session we, as psychologists, listen to how the person speaks about the tedious testing experience. These words often describe quite well how the A-D/HD individual experiences their own attentional deficits.

As psychologists, we never recommend diagnosing A-D/HD in the first testing session. Instead, we seek to rule-out several diagnoses and to conduct a Differential Diagnosis. Individual's often come to the office seeking a second opinion, since so many children and adolescents are often misdiagnosed, and are then placed on medication by pediatricians doing the best that they can within the time they have to work with a child. However, the working pair of a pediatrician who can prescribe medication if necessary and a psychologist who can conduct testing and individual and/or family psychotherapy is an excellent Therapeutic Treatment Team to effectively treat the physiological and psychological components of the A-D/HD patient. Hence, many pediatricians also refer their patients to a psychologist for confirmation of the diagnosis of A-D/HD. Communication between the Treatment Team is essential for the maximum therapeutic progress and a positive prognosis.

CHAPTER 5

Projective Tests in Differential Diagnosis

Although research may not yet support this view, many psychologists emphasize the utilization of projective technique with A-D/HD individuals, since we are looking at a differential diagnosis factor. The House-Tree-Person Test (HTP), Kinetic Family Drawing, and other Projective Drawings help to rule-out other aspects of anxiety and/or depression. We ask the patient to draw: (a) a house, (b) a tree, and (c) a whole person from head to toe, the best person they can realistically draw. In later psychotherapy sessions they are also asked to draw a person of the opposite sex than that of the first person. Each specific drawing pulls for additional, affective information. In the Kinetic Family Drawing a hypothesis can often be made regarding the relationships within the family. Another example is that by using a Person in the Rain projective drawing we can assess the patient's vulnerability factor. If a child is depressed, anxious, and/or grandiose, we are often looking at a budding bipolar disorder, oppositional defiant disorder, overanxious disorder of childhood, and many other different possibilities.

During the projective assessment we also ask the subject to draw their favorite animal, by saying, "If you had to be an animal, what would it be?" Then we ask them to draw a second animal that they would never ever want to be. This sometimes expresses a person's valued or unacceptable personality factors from that individual's point of view. Thereby, we assess personality factors that the person being tested may not consciously be trying to project. The Telephone Pole drawing, believed initially to be from

Temple University, can reflect perceptions of body anxiety, and functionality. We ask our patients to draw the "Worst Possible Thing You Can Ever Imagine Happening". They are also asked to draw a picture of themselves, and to then write down three wishes, anything in the world that if they wished it, it would come true. The Personality Orientation Device, also believed to be from Temple University, was not used widely, but was presented by Dr. Spero at the Florida Psychological Association Summer Convention in the past. Whatever an individual draws says something about their personality functioning. Lines drawn coming in a downward direction toward the self may indicate a level of depression. The quadrants in the paper can theoretically reflect attitudes about one's mother and father, and how the individual relates to their own environment. A second administration of the assessment technique then looks at either a preservative quality, or if the patient is able to produce a totally different pattern. For each of the projective drawings, we then ask questions such as, "How old is the tree and how does the tree feel?" We look to the subject's own description of their pictures drawn.

The Person in the Rain Drawing has been incredibly valuable clinically in that we have gained a lot of information about how individuals deal with adversity, as well as whether they have gained well developed emotional systems of defense mechanisms, and whether or not the family dynamics are evident, but not yet mentioned. A lot of time, in juvenile delinquents we could see an umbrella drawn off to one side, as the rain has been is pouring down on the person. Sometimes we see a closed umbrella being held in a downward position. Other times a hand is drawn behind the back as the individual has said that the umbrella is behind the person. The Person in the Rain Drawing when used with the Department of Children and Families in Florida, the delinquent and foster children population, or the severely emotionally disturbed individuals, have often provided more information than the House-Tree-Person Test. Although we have not yet seen a lot of normative data, the information is very useful clinically, and we strongly recommend that all psychologists, for the purpose of differential diagnosis and assessing affective factors, consider this additional form of data gathering as part of their own A-D/HD Psychological Evaluations.

As psychologists we look at the objectively scored tests first, yet we also rely heavily upon our ability to be humanistic psychologists and to use other Projective Personality Tests such as the Sentence Completion Test. However, it is important that the evaluating psychologist spend as much time as possible with the subject, as he/she administers each test. Breaks in testing in which spontaneous conversation begins often provides much needed additional information. So much can be learned during testing sessions, by using basic psychological instincts.

In terms of intellectual assessment tools, we recommend utilizing the following the WISC-V, Wechsler Intelligence Scale for Children-Fifth Edition, the WIAT-II, Wechsler Individual Achievement Test-Third Edition, and for perceptual motor development: The Bender Visual Motor Gestalt Test-II. In years to come, each of the revised versions of these tests may still prove to be helpful in the process of psychological evaluation of A-D/HD individuals.

A thorough Diagnostic Interview with the child or adolescent, often results in the patient saying that nobody actually had ever asked them questions directly. Instead, the informational sessions by other Psychologists were overly focused upon the parents providing all of the information. Dialog with the child or adolescent is essential, they often have a desire for someone to listen to them. They may need the structure or help in answering the questions one by one, and for you and them as well to participate in the process of differential diagnosis and treatment decision making. Hence, we have almost always found it to be therapeutic to administer the self-rating scale for children and adolescents, along with one or more of the Continuous Performance Tests.

CHAPTER 6

Continuous Performance Tests

While working with N.I.M.H., National Institute of Mental Health, Mirsky was involved with a project that seemed to be critical of the current commercially available continuous performance tests because they present stimuli on a randomized sequence. The interval of time between stimuli changes. There are also some other complaints about the commercially available tests. However, the other tests, which are being used in the current N.I.M.H. research projects, are not yet commercially available. At this point in time we have to rely upon our current instruments until these other tests have been further developed and eventually published for use in the field of psychology.

Regardless, the use of more than one Continuous Performance Test in the process of diagnosing A-D/HD is extremely effective. These tests are accurate to one thousandth of a second, and add so much useful information to the process of assessment for A-D/HD. In many cases it would not be considered good practice to diagnose A-D/HD without first administering a Continuous Performance Test. As licensed psychologists, we evaluate a lot of second opinion cases of children and adolescents who have been diagnosed with one disorder or another. Referrals often reveal that the original diagnosis was incorrect because a treatment plan had not been effective, and also much of the time, because the evaluators had not included Continuous Performance Tests. It is sad to say, but often an entire assessment had to be readministered. If the assessment had been completed recently, we would try to let that assessment stand, and instead add some additional neuropsychological components by using some of the Continuous Performance Tests, and some of the projective techniques to rule-out or to confirm the diagnosis of A-D/HD.

At the time that this book was written, there was at least three or four Continuous Performance Tests available commercially. The approximate cost for the startup of each computer testing location for a Psychologist's office varies between $300-$600. The CPT-II Conners' Continuous Performance Test-II, is one of the tests that is quite user friendly, even if the evaluator is not computer literate. It provides a readable Test Summary, accompanied by many charts and graphs which can be given to parents and pediatricians. Parents may still need an explanation, but having a readable print-out helps parents to understand the level and severity of the disorder. Pediatricians and psychologists also appreciate the computer generated test results, in that the report adds validity for administering medication when deemed necessary.

The TOVA-8, Test of Variables of Attention, Version 8, which is in extensive use and has a solid history and research background, provides a visual and auditory assessment for comparison. In contrast, the Conners' Continuous Performance Test-II (V.5) is only a visual continuous performance test. However, it may seem difficult to read the TOVA-8 printout at first and, it cannot be handed to parents without a thorough explanation as it is mostly numbers and quartile scores, with minimal written text explanation. Psychologists may also need additional training and supervised experience to completely understand it. A clear reading of the computer-generated printout requires knowledge of the test itself. Nonetheless, the computer generated report does include a concise statement summary in which A-D/HD is either suggested or viewed not to be evident in the data.

Communicating test findings to the treating pediatrician, psychiatrist, or pediatric neurologist when the test results are not within normal limits and are suggestive of an attention disorder, is made easier in that one section of the TOVA-8 computer printout clearly identifies A-D/HD. Providing this type of concrete, objectively scored test data with a computer generated, printed report to the physician is a crucial link in the Treatment Team effort between the medical physician and the psychologist.

The following quote comes from the Conners' CPT-II (V.5), and provides the exact percentage of psychopathology. For example, the test results are: "68.3% more likely to match a clinical profile as compared to a non-clinical profile." These computer-generated pages give the medical physician something concrete to place into their records, and if they then choose to prescribe medication, they are able to do so at that time knowing that they have documented printed evidence in their own medical chart of the diagnosis of A-D/HD.

CHAPTER 7

Case History

In our office, years ago, Dr. Michael evaluated a teenager from a private school who was having difficulty with classroom examinations and Standardized Tests while possessing a high average level of overall intelligence. We administered the Conners' CPT-II (V.5) and the results reflected a 99% likelihood to be in the category of attention deficit. We also administered the TOVA-8. The medical doctor prescribed Ritalin 5mg. The individual then increased their performance from the 37th percentile on a Standardized Test to the 89th percentile in only one month.

As psychologists, we recommend that the treating mental health professional re-administer a Continuous Performance Test during the course of the treatment to assist the prescribing physician with additional information as to whether or not the medication is working at a minimal to a maximal level of effectiveness. Physicians and Psychologists can work in close conjunction based on continuous communication occurring for the best interest of their mutual patients.

It is also important to us to help parents to recognize whether or not their children or adolescents, or if the adults themselves, have been misdiagnosed as A-D/HD. A large number of children whose parents bring them to us say that their children or adolescents must be A-D/HD because they are only getting "C's" and "D's" in school, which is often a significant decline from previous patterns of grades. These children and adolescents have often been maintained on prescription medication with little or no results in their levels of cognitive and executive functioning. With permission from the parents and/ or legal guardian, or the individual themselves, their medical doctor temporarily discontinues all psychostimulants and other medications. During this clinically determined 'drug holiday' these children, adolescents, and adults can benefit from targeted psychological treatment focusing upon motivational problems and repetition problems. With proper psychological treatment and educational intervention, organizational skills deficits often can improve. The significant improvement suggests a possible misdiagnosis of A-D/HD commonly based on poor grades and reports of attentional problems that are more motivational, organizational, or related to anxiety, depression, or oppositional defiant behavior. A second opinion is strongly recommended if the diagnosis was made without a Psychological Evaluation by a licensed psychologist.

In the psychological Treatment of A-D/HD, we strongly encourage the utilization of Structural Family Therapy, Cognitive-Behavioral Brief Individual Psychotherapy, Play Therapy, Token Economy Behavior Modification Programs, and other Behavioral Interventions. Our empathic, direct, and honest style is a self-managed approach of the individual patient learning how to take themselves seriously as someone who has an attention disorder, and then aids them in taking responsibility for their own behavior and progress in accepting their attention disorder, and to creatively develop strategies to compensate for it. More simply put, we teach A-D/HD individuals to own and manage their own behavior, and to choose not to **drift**.

We enjoy having a good time with these fascinating young patients by playing chess, checkers, cards, pool, and other games as a form of psychological treatment. When we teach a child or an adolescent how to think from the perspective of their parents and teachers this allows them to deal more effectively with conflicts in their lives. We help these children to grow cognitively, emotionally, and socially, and, in turn, we as psychologists also learn from each and every one of our patients, and then use this new knowledge to help future A-D/HD patients.

We hope that the reader understands the necessity of a Treatment Team Approach consisting of a psychologist, psychiatrist, pediatric neurologist, pediatrician, general practitioner, teachers, tutors, parents, spouses, and/or employers all working together to help these **"Drifters"** to remain on course, to succeed to their maximum capabilities in school, at work, and at home, as well as into their personal lives now and in the future perpetually.

CHAPTER 8

The Allan F. Mirsky, Ph.D., ABPP-CN Model

Mirsky's model is based on genetics and neurology. In particular, Mirsky talks about idiopathic generalized epilepsy (IGE) as having a fairly high concordance with symptoms that we often diagnose as A-D/HD. Greenberg's data has shown that IGE has a genetic component more often than not, which is distributed through the maternal line, Greenberg et al. (2000). However, this theory may run in contrast to many beliefs, especially when the father has himself previously also been appropriately diagnosed as having A-D/HD. The child then has a higher probability of being A-D/HD via, a genetic combined contribution. There does seem to be some evidence that the male gene does not transmit A-D/HD. We hope to soon be able to read that the human genome project has been completed, and that in the near future we will see more data surface on the etiology of   A-D/HD. At that time, the genetic factors will be better understood.

Mirsky talks about generalized seizure disorders as having a huge overlap with   A-D/HD. However, the most important data is that of juvenile myoclonic epilepsy (JME), which is a specific form of epilepsy that has specific similarities to A-D/HD. Next, there is temporal lobe epilepsy, which many psychologists probably have dealt with, and may have diagnosed these patients as A-D/HD. With JME in mild or moderate levels, one may not be diagnosed unless there is a stressor that leads to or creates a more apparent seizure. In life this behavior is like a type of **drifting** or zoning out, which can often be covered up or misused in a non-stressful situation. However, in moderate to severe levels, A-D/HD is often identified, and noted to be somewhat different than a petit mal seizure, which is usually evident in terms of a lapse of attention, and is generally identified, and triggered by an external stimuli or external state. JME however, has some identifiable differences. The continuing research of the NIMH study is available as one of the most innovative site studies on A-D/HD. Other data, according to Mirsky has shown that JME is inherited in the maternal line. Also, JME is one form of IGE (Idiopathic Generalized Epilepsy). There are other forms. Dr. Allan Mirsky's Model also includes a breakdown of various functions of the brain. He talks about the following processes: the ability of focus, execute, sustain, encode, as well as the cognitive shifting of function.

In the future, we believe that certain kinds of batteries of tests used in research will be able to specifically identify one's ability to function without cognitive interruption. From this perspective A-D/HD is then essentially viewed as being a focus disruption or a cognitive shifting disruption. By utilizing neuropsychological tests that measure these specific behaviors which are linked to specific brain areas, we can now more accurately diagnose A-D/HD. In the future, we hope that a deeper and wider based understanding of neuropsychology will be required coursework in psychology graduate school programs.

Dr. Allan Mirsky links the abilities to focus, shift, and encode to different and specific areas of the brain. However, even encoding which is a very global function, may not be as easy to specifically tie to only one particular brain area. Nevertheless, if A-D/HD individuals have trouble with visual, auditory, or kinesthetic encoding, then these problems can point to a particular brain lobe. When we talk about a particular type of attention, we are looking at one's ability to focus, and then to follow through with the execution of a task. In a functional specialization, we are talking about encoding. Next, we ask, how do we incorporate this information, and how do we bring this information into the A-D/HD person's world. The A-D/HD individual may have trouble expressing themselves in that their behavioral pattern of rushing ahead, or appearing to be out of sequence in the completion of a task is quite frustrating for the A-D/HD individuals. This area of research dates back to the 1950's in theory. Rosvold, et al. (1956) was noting the relationship between brain injury and impaired attention in several populations.

More recently however, Greenberg et al. (2000) have been able to point out that the locus on human chromosome number six may contain basically the juvenile myoclonic epilepsy chromosome. With the identification of chromosome number six, for the first time we actually have a genetic marker related to A-D/HD. Hence, psychological and medical aspects are finally being blended in the identification and treatment of A-D/HD individuals.

A good deal of Mirsky's work does involve the relationship between impaired attention and epilepsy, but an equivalent portion of this research has focused on schizophrenia and the relatives of schizophrenics. The research is pretty conclusive that the first degree relatives of schizophrenics, have many representations that are consistent with attention deficits and some seizure activities, Mirsky et al. (1995). Mirsky is not claiming that A-D/HD is a form of epilepsy, because it is not corroborated at this time with the data that we currently have, but all the evidence seems to be pointing in that direction. The premise, although not completely revolutionary can really change how we conceptualize the specific needs of these individuals. Most parents would not refuse to treat their children with medication if their child were to be diagnosed with epilepsy by a neurologist. Yet, there is often resistance among parents to utilize medication as a form of treatment for A-D/HD, despite the fact that the data supports the physiological need in specific cases. This is also applicable to adolescents and adults.

Current research has stopped just short of proving that A-D/HD is some form of a brain seizure disorder. The data suggests there are neurological dysfunctions in A-D/HD patients that are almost, totally ameliorated by pharmacological intervention in some cases. Parents usually ask us as psychologists if they will be referred to a medical physician for a medication consult. We agree that severe cases should be referred to pediatricians or to psychiatrists, but not all A-D/HD cases require medication. Nevertheless, once we explain to parents that A-D/HD is a medical condition rather than just a learned behavioral pattern of functioning, they seem to be somewhat more likely to consider psychological treatment combined with medication. Nonetheless, we estimate that only 60% of the A-D/HD patients that we treat require psychopharmacological treatment. However, A-D/HD is not something that a child will outgrow.

Mirsky stated that the first-degree relatives of schizophrenics may share inattention problems in milder forms, which is a specific area that no one else to our knowledge has yet proven. A-D/HD chromosome abnormality is a new concept for most parents. There is treatment for A-D/HD which addresses the behavior components, but there is also undoubtedly a medical factor present. In addition, first degree relatives have a strong concordance, that there is some related neurological behavior that is dysfunctional. However, this has been found to be true in second and third degree relatives, and in identical twins. In the late Dr. Michael's research, she notes that Schizophrenia has a pretty high concordance of .06-.07. However, this is not found to be true in identical twins, or even fraternal twins, cousins, and aunts and uncles. Therefore, taking an extensive and thorough family history becomes extremely important in the process of a Diagnostic Interview. The linkage to schizophrenia was not one that we have made. Furthermore, it seems that no one had made this connection until the data started corroborating this hypothesis. Much is yet to be learned in the field with regard to these theories.

When psychologists take the time with the parent without the child or adolescent present, and complete the Medical/Developmental background information section of the Diagnostic Interview, we recommend that the historical data be divided into various segments, i.e. what was the time period in which the parents were having children, was the pregnancy planned or unplanned, were there any types of complication during labor and/or delivery, and finally was there a low birth weight and if so, why? When a mother says that the child was premature, then other factors must be considered. For example, we ask: Were you aware that you were pregnant? What actually happened during that time? Did you smoke, consume alcohol, or was there any form of substance abuse? How could that have affected the in-vitro development of the neurological system? Attention deficits may have various etiologies. Hence, a thorough Diagnostic Interview is an essential component of effectively diagnosing A-D/HD.

*Allan F. Mirsky, Ph.D., ABBP-CN personally edited this chapter about his Model of A-D/HD.

CHAPTER 9

The Russell Barkley, M.D. approach to A-D/HD:

Russell Barkley, M.D. is a very respected researcher in the evaluation and treatment of A-D/HD. However, in his most recent work which advocates a neurological psychology approach to A-D/HD, there is no mention of the Luria Model. However, in 1998 at his seminar in South Florida, with humor intended, he did mention the fabulous cartoonist Gary Larson. The specific slide was that of a young boy looking at his shoes, who was simply repeating over and over, "Socks first, then shoes. Socks first, then shoes." This sarcastic portrayal of A-D/HD children's and adolescent's behavior brings a smile to one's face.

In his film "A-D/HD WHAT CAN WE DO ABOUT IT?" Dr. Barkley seemed to be almost too harsh in his approach of telling the parents that their child has a form of brain damage. Rather than focusing on the physiological approach, let us now turn to the behavioral component of the diagnosis, and the history of the Diagnostic and Statistical Manual of the American Psychiatric Association: DSM-II, DSM-III, DSM-III-R, DSM-IV, DSM-IV TR, and DSM-5/ ICD-10, and see how many different diagnoses we have had over the years for the same condition. If you brought your child to a psychologist in 1979, the diagnosis was said to be Minimal Brain Dysfunction. Now, who wants to go through life telling people, "The reason I don't listen to you, is because I have Minimal Brain Dysfunction. I would like to apply for a job or at least attempt to have relationships, but I have a dysfunctional brain." What an outrageous diagnostic label! Next, we classified ADD, With or Without Hyperactivity.

This diagnosis took a long time for parents and professionals to say. So, are we currently working on shortening the diagnosis for parents and children as well? Time will tell. However, the diagnostic categories currently involve Attention-Deficit/Hyperactivity Disorder Combined Presentation, Predominantly Inattentive Presentation, Predominantly Hyperactive/Impulsive Presentation, and Unspecified Attention-Deficit/Hyperactivity Disorder.

On a more serious note, Barkley talks about disinhibiting as being the primary factor of A-D/HD. When we talk about a disinhibitory disorder, we address how the child internally processes internalization of language, reconstitution, neurobiological self-control issues, focusing of attention, and encoding. Next, we assess how they make sense in the world, or more specifically how do they let you know that they actually understand what is going on with regard to their level of impulsivity, the hyper-verbal aspects, the inattention, or all of these factors combined. We say that A-D/HD is not specifically a filtering disorder. Behaviors that should be inhibited are released. It is not just an attention deficit; it is a response disorder, and that is why we measure A-D/HD with Continuous Performance Tests and projective tests, as well as cognitive measures of intellectual functioning. As psychologists, when we talk of a full-battery of psychological tests we will administer a WISC-V (Wechsler Intelligence Scale for Children-Fifth Edition), a full standardized achievement test, and several personality measures. By utilizing the DSM-5 (ICD-10) we assess Depression, Anxiety, Bipolar Disorder, Oppositional Defiant Disorder, Specific Learning Disabilities, Tourette's Disorder, and many other aspects of adjustment such as divorce, death in the family, moving, bullying at school, poor grades, and any other issues that can affect a child. Again, A-D/HD not just a processing problem, but an incorporation of many various factors. Hence, these individuals almost always need a mixture of psychopathologic therapy, and they intermittently need our help as licensed psychologists over an extended period of time. To this end, we should all remember Nicholas Cumming, Ph.D.'s 1988 terminology of "brief-intermittent psychotherapy throughout the life cycle". If this is an area in which a psychologist chooses to specialize, then they truly become an important part of helping many A-D/HD children, adolescents, and adults. As psychologists, we may not see these patients for half a year, or two to three years, or even more, but they do often come back to the office for continued interpersonal growth and assistance at the time of various developmental crises.

Barkley's approach seemed to describe A-D/HD as a response inhibition. It is a disinhibitory function, a frontal lobe function. This is not in opposition to Luria's perspective. As previously stated, both individuals may be correct. The one thing that is sure however, is that the various conflictual beliefs with regard to the etiology and the evaluation and treatment of A-D/HD continue to exist in the research, and also in our practices as well, as licensed psychologists.

CHAPTER 10

Risk Factors of
Attention-Deficit/Hyperactivity Disorder:

Gestational problems, premature birth and toxemia, and family history are all important to assess in A-D/HD. Misdiagnosed learning disabilities may have actually been an unrecognized attention disorder in people who are only one generation prior to that of the child. In past generations, the mental health professionals often did not identify A-D/HD individuals. In the 1970's, we started looking deeper into Specific Learning Disabilities. However, many of those children may have been undiagnosed A-D/HD. The neurological history is important to assess, especially considering the data from Mirsky, who looks at the concordance of A-D/HD with epilepsy, schizophrenia, and depression.

Depression

Depression can overlap with A-D/HD. Many children who have A-D/HD are also depressed. The depression can be secondary and concomitant. They always seem to be developmentally slow or late to develop, and nobody is really completely satisfied with their behavior. Parents and teachers often correct and sometimes even scold them for their behavior. They may feel sad, angry, inadequate, frustrated and rejected. Low levels of self-esteem may be the result of these feelings. Hence, many A-D/HD children are depressed. They actually experience a reactive depression, which in turn further affects their ability to concentrate. Furthermore, some children and adolescents may mask their sadness with displays of anger. Structure and consistency in parenting skills are essential. Maternal depression whether during gestation, during the early years of a child's life, or later in childhood can also significantly affect the child's emotional development.

Anxiety

Anxiety disorders are also known to have a genetic component and can also be present as an attention disorder. When people are anxious their ability to maintain focus or concentration may be affected. They may drift and focus on internal stimuli or other irrelevant details. Hence, some children who are misdiagnosed as A-D/HD are really coping with an anxiety disorder. However, A-D/HD and anxiety can also be concomitant. This is especially true when the A-D/HD individual worries about their past or future behaviors and their effects upon others.

Alcohol and Substance Abuse

We must also assess alcohol and/or other substance abuse or dependency, particularly in the males of our culture. A lot of people with A-D/HD self-medicate with alcohol and other substances that can lead to addiction. The genome issues may come out that these are related to added functions as well. As psychologists, we believe that parents
can sometimes underestimate the importance of life circumstances or stress factors. Life stress factors must be addressed for the A-D/HD individual and taken into account. Those emotions can affect one's ability to concentrate.

Environmental Factors

Next, we must consider environmental risk factors, such as domestic discord. We are living in times that are disruptive with domestic violence. Many children are exposed to parental arguments at home. Therefore, when the children go to school, they are often easily distracted or preoccupied with thoughts of their home environment. Hence, they may not have an attention disorder at all. If environmental issues are disorganized or inconsistent this can add to the stress for the child or adolescent.

We find a large percentage of our patients who are more on the behavioral than the neurological deficit side, were often raised by an aunt or a grandmother for several years, then they moved to their mother or the home of another relative, or were watched by someone who had a completely differently parenting style. Structure and consistency of discipline is essential for maximal interpersonal communication skills development. As psychologists, we recommend firm, consistent, and empathic limit setting.

When we assess depression we must also consider the physiological components of the chemistry of the brain, such as dopamine, serotonin and norepinephrine levels. When we look at attentional aspects we must rule-out anxiety and depression. A child who is A-D/HD and overanxious, will at times actually perform better on some of the Continuous Performance Tests, because they are so anxious that they are actually attempting to be hyper vigilant. Hence, they are trying not to miss any responses and this factor makes it very difficult to assess emotionally affected concentration difficulties vs. inattentiveness. We recommend a thorough full-battery Psychological Evaluation and differential diagnosis over a period of several testing sessions. Many of us see children where the parent is pressuring us to give the child the answer to their problems in the first session.   However, it is acceptable to say that we have a preliminary or a working diagnosis, and we will do some testing, and then we will explain to the parents and child or adolescent what is going on over a period of time, and not just inattention or distractibility as a result of anxiety and/or depression.

If we talk about a predisposition, we can recognize that with some medical conditions, such as diabetes or a heart condition, the extent of the illness is often linked to exposure of significant levels of stress. A-D/HD is not brought on by stress, and the symptoms are generally present by age seven. Yet, the symptoms can actually be exacerbated by other life stress producing situations such as being bullied, academic difficulties or failure, an overlay with regard to any type of learning disability, depression, anxiety, or even simple and complex factors of adjustment. Some parents of our young patients may state their child probably always had A-D/HD, but they did not see it prior to a particular episode or life experience. Others will claim that at two years old their child did not sleep, and they knew that there was something going on with the excessive level of energy. Some parents remember the exact moment of how their child or children even climbed out of their crib, and were later found down the street before the parents even knew where their children were. The A-D/HD toddler or young child needs constant supervision. Groups, such as CHADD, Children with Attention Deficit Disorder, can provide a support system for these families.

CHAPTER 11

A Current View of
Attention- Deficit/Hyperactivity Disorder
Symptoms of Inattention

With regard to the DSM-5/ICD-10 criteria for A-D/HD, many children forget things, and very few typical children or teens really want to stop playing to do their homework. The question then is, "What is the difference between the A-D/HD child and the child who does not have A-D/HD?" For this answer, we must assess the level of disruption to their life duties, their ability to function, and their level of disruptive behaviors. After a thorough assessment it seems quite clear that psychological or psychiatric treatment may be medically necessary. These debilitating behaviors encompass symptoms of inattention, but they also include symptoms of impulsivity and hyperactivity. The impulsive and hyperactive child is more likely to go into the pediatrician's office or clinic earlier, because their parents find that their child is having difficulty controlling his or her behavior at a very young age. Some of these children do have dangerous impulses such as; darting out into traffic, or the grabbing of sharp instruments. These children seem to have a disinhibitory problem. These are the kinds of children that the Barkley Model seems to manage very well, because there is no question that there is a Disinhibitory Disorder. If the child is falling behind others, and is not functioning well socially or academically then psychological and/or psychiatric treatment may be necessary. However, an inattentive child who does not have a hyperactive or impulsive nature, does not seem to be as clearly explained by the Barkley Model. As a matter of fact, these individuals are often not going to come into our office for the most part until the middle of grade school, unless they have a severe condition. They are rarely diagnosed before the age of seven, and sometimes as late as pre-adolescence, or even as teenagers or young adults. This is one of the reasons that DSM-5 will eventually be redefined in the DSM-5/ICD-10. Many children will often do pretty well except that, they will at unpredictable times just zone out, or **drift**. They will do well in school, they engage in their own activities, they are often fairly bright, and they will have no problem in grade school until they reach the fourth grade and they have to complete mathematics such as multi-step multiplication problems and/or long division problems. Whenever they have a complex math problem to perform an internalization consolidation problem may begin to be evident. Yet, if they are very bright, they may get through simple division and then, they will often hit a lull in middle school, and be diagnosed later in high school.

Unfortunately, these children are likely to be misdiagnosed or overlooked by parents who believe that adolescence involves an enormous amount of hormones that disrupt everything including concentration. Now, there are normal hormonal changes that occur in adolescence, but promulgating the myth that all adolescents are anxious, despondent, or impulsive does not allow for parents or teachers to look favorably at the child or teenager's behavior. Very often these are undiagnosed attention deficit disorders. When we ask them why they came in to our offices, or why their grades are low, or how do they conceptualize their problem, they are confused and cannot seem to pin point reasons for the problems at home and/or at school. They are simply overwhelmed, and **drifting**.

In assessing these types of cases, we use the Conners'-Wells' Adolescent Self Report Scale: Long Version, by C. Keith Conners', Ph.D. and Staff. We also generally have the parents and the child or adolescent in the room as we overview the diagnostic criterion. We also take the time separately with the child for Play Therapy as part of the process of the assessment. Direct Observation is an integral component of our understanding of the child's behavioral patterns and emotions.

The approximate estimate of children with A-D/HD in the common population is 13% or thirteen out of one hundred people. While looking at children from the ages seven to nine, 3 to 5% of boys and 1 to 3% of girls are appropriately diagnosed with A-D/HD. This makes boys are four times as likely to be diagnosed A-D/HD.

Oppositional Defiant Disorder

Another important function to assess is O.D.D., Oppositional Defiant Disorder. One in forty-eight O.D.D. children were also A-D/HD, and 65% of A-D/HD children according to Dr. Barkley were also diagnosed Oppositional Deficient Disorder. O.D.D. This is not the type of diagnosis that only specifically looks at impulsivity. A lot of the behavioral symptoms of O.D.D. are seemingly intelligently planned manipulations. When we look at a child that is overanxious and also O.D.D., who is also having what we would consider as the neurobiology or self-control problem, we are going to conduct on-going differential diagnosis in Psychological Evaluation and in Psychotherapy.

Fewer girls present A-D/HD because often their symptoms are less aggressive in nature. This is the case because they are often under diagnosed, being less likely to be impulsive, due to socialized suppression of aggressive behavior dating back to the time when they were very young. Much data shows that parents are gender specific in raising their children. Girls are often taught to inhibit aggressive and impulsive responses from the time that they are toddlers, whereas boys are allowed and encouraged to be more outspoken and aggressive. Hence, the boys are more likely to exhibit A-D/HD symptoms earlier on, and to a more severe level than girls. However, when A-D/HD shows up in girls, they are more likely to be more severe cases. Also, in terms of A-D/HD with hyperactivity or impulsivity, girls are less likely to be identified because they are often seen to be quieter than boys in grade or middle school. Furthermore, girls very often, at this age, have stronger verbal skills, which may also help them to compensate. This is of particular concern in misdiagnosing females in late to middle childhood. A lot of work is needed in schools in further educating teachers how to identify a need for assessing girls, when they are **drifting** or zoning out. Increased referrals often occur after we speak with teachers and guidance counselors. Outreach into the schools is imperative to provide education to teachers, and with Dr. Spero's logic: *"If you have healthier teachers you have a healthier world. Teachers often have the greatest effect on our children. They spend many hours with our children, five days per week."*

As psychologists and parents, we must think of how many hours each day that teachers are with our children, and how much of an influence they have on our children. Dr. Spero's Psychological Doctoral Research Project was entitled, "A Needs Analysis Survey on The Burnout Phenomenon of Elementary School Teachers," with the goal of helping as many children as possible by helping their teachers. When we conduct this type of research and we go into schools, we are assisting teachers, and in turn helping children as well. One happy and healthy teacher can change a life time of memories for at least twenty-thirty children each year.

We also look at the age and needs of the children that we test. By the time a child enters fourth grade, the rate of new vocabulary words increases so rapidly that their visual skills cannot compensate as they had in the earlier grades. For example, we look at the word "boat" and we read it as boat without actually sounding it out phonetically such as b...o...a...t. By the time children enter fourth grade, there is much more classwork and homework. Many of the A-D/HD boys lag behind, so they tend to act-out behaviorally, and then they are finally referred for psychological evaluation and/or treatment. Some A-D/HD girls may not be properly diagnosed early on, but in middle school they may become depressed or anxious because they know that they are not being accepted or fitting in with their classmates. They feel different, but they can't explain it, or put into words what they are thinking and feeling. They might say something like, "I don't know, I feel like I have a hole in my brain. I just can't focus. I don't know why the other girls will not pay attention to me." Adolescents can be so vicious at that age, so when the other girls tease the A-D/HD teenager and call them names, there may be an exacerbation of depression leading to further internal focusing and inattention. Other children and teenagers will tease them, and as victims they may remember this bullying, humiliation, and helplessness for the rest of their lives. So, when we see these children and teenagers in psychotherapy, we often make a difference not only at that moment, but from that point on as we also gradually work our way back into the development of self-esteem and the formation of the personality.

C. Keith Conners, Ph.D. emphasized that the main thing we have going for us is the level of trust that we, as psychologists, can provide, and that these A-D/HD children and teenagers have often not yet completely trusted any adults other than their family members. Therefore, they do not have a sense of hope. So, if we can instill hope, trust, and bonding as the main part of the therapeutic experience, we know we have done a lot for these young patients. Although we are emphasizing the biological and physiological aspects, we also want to emphasize the importance of the humanistic aspects of psychological treatment. The relationship between the A-D/HD individual and their psychologist is of the utmost importance.

Some symptoms causing impairment are often not evident before the age of seven. Many undiagnosed A-D/HD children without hyperactivity are often misdiagnosed. Unless the A-D/HD individual's condition is moderate to severe, as previously stated, they may not necessarily be identified be teachers, parent, or significant adults in their lives.

There are currently three different diagnostic specifiers of A-D/HD that are defined by the DSM-5. These three categories are best used for children and adolescents in the diagnosis of Attention-Deficit/Hyperactivity Disorder. Not Otherwise Specified, or NOS, is a fourth A-D/HD diagnosis which is primarily used with adults. These individuals do not have the specificity of meeting the seven-year-old criteria by self-report in the absence of their parents and as a child may or may not have met the criteria of the symptomatology being present prior to the age of seven years old.

It is also best to use the category of being Unspecified A-D/HD when there are multiple other vague neurological impairments, because we cannot really specify which aspect of attention may be due to one neurological factor of impairing or exacerbating concentrated problem at one time. The key is not to diagnose on the presenting symptoms alone, but also when possible to bring in past history as presented by other individuals who knew this person as a child. When the adult completes the Conners'-3 Self-Report Scale, he or she should complete the self-report measures knowing that they are out of the norms, and hence the age norms can be adjusted so as to present a high school mindset. For adults completing self-report forms, they are asked to respond as they saw themselves as adolescents and as children. Hence, by utilizing this form of a self-report we are in keeping with the philosophy of C. Keith Conners, Ph.D. who strongly emphasized the importance of taking a complete developmental history.

One of the things that makes A-D/HD diagnosis difficult is that there are a lot of situational variables. It is often commented on by parents, that if their child is intrinsically motivated to attend to something such as a TV program or to video games, that the child can sustain attention in some tasks for long periods of time. Many parents are confused by this phenomenon. However, it can be understood that because so much is happening on the TV, computer, tablet, or cellphone screen, the child seems to be vicariously experiencing a high level of arousal, activity, and energy.

With regard to family dynamics, there is also data indicating that symptoms are often expressed or acted-out more in the presence of the mother than with the father, probably because when many children are with their fathers there may be a stronger inhibition. The father may spend less time with the child than the mother and may be more of a disciplinary model, even if they are not even viewed to be a disciplinarian. Our own data has often shown that the fathers say that they do not see the same symptoms as the children's mothers. This may cause discord between the husband and wife, because husbands might blame their wives for not controlling the negative impulsive and disruptive behaviors of their children. This may prove to be particularly true in divorced households. In those cases, we believe that it is best to administer the CPRS-R:L, Conners'-3 Parent Rating Scale-Revised: Long Version, by each parent separately without collaboration between the parents. Having the father complete the rating scale separately, then comparing the results to the mother's computer generated report, and next by comparing both of these to the teacher report forms, as well as including the other data gathered, is the strongest basis on which to make an A-D/HD behavioral diagnosis. It is also very effective for the psychologist to go out to the school and to observe the children in their own school environment. This observation experience is almost always worth the time, effort, and expense of travel.

In school and at home, if children get one-on-one attention and specific instruction, they often do not show the same extent of cognitive disruption. There are situational variations to assess, but we do not exclude any of these factors and their effect upon the observation session. We always recommend in an A-D/HD assessment battery of psychological tests, that the patient have a current physical exam, which must include a medical and neurological history, if there has been any neurological indications or impairments from the time of birth. We also routinely communicate directly with the neurologist, psychiatrist, pediatrician, and primary care physician to maintain a unified and consistent Treatment Team approach.

If there is any reported history of seizures or convulsions, we request copies of the lab work if it has been completed, and strongly suggest all treating psychologists to request and verify with as much specificity about seizures, and medical treatment; what occurred, and if there are any discrepancies in the medical records. By gathering this information, the frequency of a link to Monochromic Epilepsy could, in the future, be validated.

Many different medications can cause disruptions in attention. Certain kinds of treatment for asthma, specifically antihistamines, may also cause behavior that directly overlaps or mimics some of the hyperactive and impulsive symptoms we see in A-D/HD. Hence, a thorough medical history is an essential element to the Diagnostic Interview. A developmental history, prior academic documentation of problematic grades or behavior, and a complete parental history is also absolutely essential.

We also want to know everything about gestation. Gestational integrity does have an impact on the prevalence of further in vitro neurological impairment and the future behavior of the A-D/HD individual. Information regarding birth and parental history for the first four weeks after birth are also essential. We may even request birth records. We want to know if that specific child had pulmonary insufficiency, brain damage, trauma, jaundice, or anoxic damage during these first few months of life. We also request school records, report cards, and IEP's: Individual Educational Plans. Many parents come in with a thick folder much of which becomes part of our own files. We personally want to know situational triggers which can be behavioral, but also can be related to neurological functioning. People do experience seizures in certain kinds of situations, i.e. when they are hungry, tired, or have not had enough sleep. A well-developed A-D/HD symptom log can often reflect specific patterns of functioning, and a wealth of other information.

Finally, it's important to know that if you or a loved one has A-D/HD, or may have A-D/HD, there are many resources available. Attention-Deficit/Hyperactivity Disorder is a manageable condition. This publication is the second in a long line of future books and games dedicated to understanding and managing mental health and happiness. The first book and game, "Florida The Turtle Who Thinks He's a Dog Finds His Feelings", was written for the children and young teenagers struggling to overcome anxiety, fears, and shyness and to further develop a feelings words vocabulary. In contrast, "Attention-Deficit/Hyperactivity Disorder, A Guide to Testing, Diagnosis, and Treatment for Drifters in a Squirrel Moment" is not only for those whose minds drift away to unimportant thoughts, like squirrels, but also for those who want to understand the ones they love who are diagnosed with A-D/HD. Florida the Turtle says that he has never had a drifter's, squirrel moment. As a matter of fact, "Turtle Talk" will, in the future, explain this interesting phenomena.

Look out for new books and games in the future
by Stable Life, L.L.C. / Dr. Mitch Spero
and Florida The Turtle Who Thinks He's a Dog

For additional publications of Games and Books by Dr. Mitch Spero/Stable Life, L.L.C. go to:
www.citiofbooks.com

You can find Dr. Mitch Spero's other books and games at
www.FloridaTheTurtle.com

Florida The Turtle Who Thinks He's A Dog Finds His Feelings/A book to help your child to Overcome Anxiety, Fears and Shyness, and to find, understand and share their feelings!

APPENDIX

CPT- Continuous Performance Tests:
*All are normed by age and gender
Provide information about Initial and Sustained Attention
Sequence 1, 2, and 4 seconds on a random presentation of stimulus, (sometimes the stimulus is flashing quickly, moderately or very slowly)
From our experience there are very few false positives, and only some false negatives.
Criterion for a positive indication is two standard deviations from the mean.

Composite of Co-morbidity with A-D/HD:
* Anxiety Disorder
* Depression
* Learning Disabilities
* Oppositional Defiant Disorder
* Conduct Disorder
* Bipolar Disorder
* Eating Disorder
* Substance and Alcohol Abuse or Dependence
* Enuresis
* Tourette's Disorder
* And More...

Medication and/or Psychological Treatments:
    Evidence points to a neurological basis of A-D/HD and a medication effectiveness in approximately 60% of our own

patients. Dr. Barkley, in his previously mentioned seminar in South Florida in 1994, stated that 95% of A-D/HD patients required medication with an efficacy rate of 60-70% of improvement during treatment. One difference between medication and cognitive-behavioral intervention is that when medication stops, the effect may also end. Where as in psychological treatment the result may last in perpetuity.

Recommended Treatment of A-D/HD:
*Play Therapy
*Cognitive-Behavioral Brief Psychotherapy
*Structural Family Therapy
* Educational Intervention
* Psychological Evaluation and Treatment
* Multimodal Comprehensive Treatments
* Education (of the teachers, parents, adolescents, children, and other family members)
* Behavioral Management/Behavior Modification Token Economy Systems
* Medical Management / Psychopharmacological Treatment
* Listening and Responding to the needs of the A-D/HD individual
* Continuous Communication
*Read our book again and share it with others...

Thank You!

RECOMMENDED A-D/HD ASSESSMENT TECHNIQUES

Wechsler Intelligence Scale for Children – Fifth Edition (WISC-5)
Conners' Continuous Performance Test-II CPT-II – Version 5 (CPT-II)
T.O.V.A.-8 - Test of Variables of Attention – Version 8 (TOVA-8)
House-Tree-Person #1 Test (HTP) and Person #2
Kinetic Family Drawing (KFD)
Person in The Rain
Other Projective Drawings
§   Favorite Animal and Least Favorite Animal
§   Telephone Pole
§   Worst Possible Thing You Can Imagine
§   Self (Head to toe)
§   List 3 Wishes (No drawings)
Conners 3™-Self-Report Rating Scale (C 3™-Self)
Conners 3™-Parent Rating Scale (C 3™-P) (each parent completes
      separately)
Conners 3™-Teacher Rating Scale (C 3™-T)
Rotter Incomplete Sentence Blank (SC):
§   Children's Sentence Completion Test
§   High School Sentence Completion Test
§   Adult Sentence Completion Test
Bender Visual Motor Gestalt Test (BG)
Thematic Apperception Test (TAT)
Diagnostic Interview (DI)
Individual Psychotherapy (IP)
Review of Records
School Observation
Informal Observation
Consultation with Educators and Other Family Members
Play Therapy
Structural Family Therapy
Consultation with Medical Physician

The Dr. Spero and Dr. Michael
Overview of The Key Factors of Psychologically
Evaluating and Treating A-D/HD:

What is A-D/HD?

Diagnosis
- Neurological, Behavioral, or Genetic Factors
- Bored, Lazy, or Just Doesn't Pay Attention
- Hidden Criticism About A-D/HD

The Processes That Make up A-D/HD
- Executive Function: "I'll pay attention, plan, and execute the instructions, Sir! vs. "What did you just say to me?"
- Vigilance: "Oh boy, this is important!" vs. "Huh?"
- Distractibility: "This is interesting, now what was I doing?" vs. "Where was I?"

Sustaining vs. Selective Attention
- Sustaining Attention: "Keep paying attention, keep paying attention, keep paying attention!"
- Selective Attention: "There's so much happening, what is the most important thing to pay attention to?"

Input or Output Disorder
- A Current Question in The Research

Memory Issues in A-D/HD
- Learning Efficiency: "I did study, but I just can't remember it!"

Impulsive Behavior
- Figuring Out What's Important and Setting Priorities

The Combination of Attention-Deficit/Hyperactivity Disorder and Learning Disabilities

Theoretical Models: Aleksandr Romanovick Luria, Ph.D.
- The Luria Model
  - The Arousal and Reticular Activating System
  - The Sensory System
  - The Output and Planning System
- Donald Michenbaum, Ph.D.
  - Critique of The Luria Model

The Attention-Deficit/Hyperactivity Disorder Psychological Evaluation Process
- Projective Tests with Differential Diagnosis
- Continuous Performance Tests
- Case History

The Allan Mirsky, Ph.D. Model
The Russell Barkley, M.D. approach to A-D/HD

Risk Factors of Attention-Deficit/Hyperactivity Disorder
- Depression
- Anxiety
- Alcohol and Substance Abuse
- Environmental Factors

A Current View of Attention-Deficit/Hyperactivity Disorder
- Symptoms of Inattention
- Oppositional Defiant Disorder

References

American Psychiatric Association. (2013). Diagonstic and Statistical Manual of Mental Disorders. (5th ed.). Arlington, VA: American Psychiatric Association.

Barkley, R. A. (1994, November 7). Attention Deficit Hyperactivity Disorder in Childen and Adults. *Stonebridge Seminars*. Fort Lauderdale, FL.

Conners, C. (1992, 1995). CPT: Conners', Contuous Perforance Test. NY: Multi-Health Systems, Inc.

Conners, C. (2000). Conners' Rating Scales-Revised: Technical Manual. NY: Multi-Health Systems, Inc.

Conners, C. K. (1993, November 10). Attention Deficit Hyperactivity Disorder: Assessment and Treatment for Children and Adolescents. Fort Lauderdale, FL.

Conners, C. K. (1996, June 22-23). Attention Deficit Hyperactivity Disorder: Assessment and Treatment for Children and Adolescents. FPA Summer Convention.

Conners, C. K. (1997). Conners' Rating Scales-Revised for Windows. NY: Multi-Health Systems, Inc.

Conners, C. K. (2008). Conners 3-Parent Rating Scale. *Conners 3-Parent*. Multi-Health Systems, Inc.

Conners, C. K. (2008). Conners 3-Self-Reporting Rating Scale. *Conners 3-Self-Report*. Multi-Health Systems, Inc.

Conners, C. K. (2008). Conners 3-Teachers Rating Scale. *Conners 3-Teacher*. Multi-Health System, Inc.

Conners, C. K., & Staff. (2000). CPT-II: Continuous Performance Test II. NY: Multi-Health Systems, Inc.

Fein, A., & Fein, J. (1994). ADD: At the Cossroads. Fort Lauderdale, FL.

Greenberg, L. (2018). Test of Variables of Attention- Version 8. *T.O.V.A.* The TOVA Company.

Greenberg, D. A., Durner, M., Keddache, M., Shinnar, S., Resor, S., Moshe, S. L., Rosenbaum, D., Dicker, E. (2000). Reproductibility and complication in gene searches: Linkage on chromosome 6, heterogeneity, association, and maternal inheritance in juvenile myoclonic epilepsy. *American Journal of Human Genetics,* 66,(2), 508-516.

Horn, W. F., & Keough, C. (1999). Better Homes and Gardens: New Teen Book. Des Moines, IO: Meridith Books.

Koppitz, E. M. (1963-1973). The Bender Gestalt Test for Young Children Volume II, Research and Application. Needham, MA: Allyn and Bacon.

Koziol, L.F., Joyce, A. W., Wurglitz, G. (2014). The neuropsychology of attention: Revisiting the "Mirsky Model." *Applied Neuropsychology: Child.* http://dx.doi.org/ 10.1080/21622965.2013.870016.
(REPLICATES THE "MIRSKY MODEL." OF ELEMENTS OF ATTENTION)

Mirsky, A. (2002). National Institute of Mental Health Study. National Institute of Mental Health.

Mirsky, A. F., Anthony B. J., Duncan, C. C., Ahearn, M. B., Kellam, S. G. Analysis of the elements of attention: a neuropsychological approach. Neuropsychology Review, 1991, 2, 109-145.

Mirsky, A. F., Pascualvaca, D. M., Duncan, C. C., French, L. M. A model of attention and its relation to ADHD. Mental Retardation and Developmental Disabilities Research Reviews, 1999, 5, 169-176.

Mirsky, A. F., Yardley, S. J. Jones, B. P., Walsh, D., & Kendler, K. S. (1995). Analysis of the attention deficit in schizophrenia--A study of patients and their relatives in Ireland. *Journal of Psychiatric Research,*29, 23-42.

Parker, H. C. (1988). The ADD Hyperactivity Workbook: For Parents, Teachers, and Kids. Plantation, FL: Impact Publication.

Parker, R. N. (1992). Making the Grade: An Adolescent's Struggle With ADD. Plantation, FL: Impact Publications.

Rosvold, H. E., Mirsky, A. F., Sarason, I., Bransome, E. D. Jr., Beck, L. H. A continuous performance test of brain damage. Journal of Consulting Psychology, 1956, 20, 343-350.

Rotter, J. B. (1950). Rotter's Incomplete Sentences Completion Test. *Incomplete Sentences Blank-High School Form*, 2. The Psychological Corporation.

Rotter, J. B. (1977). Rotter Incomplete Sentences Completion Test. *Incomplete Sentences Blank-Child Form*. The Psychological Corporation.

Rotter, J. B. (1977). Rotter Incomplete Sentences Completion Test. *Incomplete Sentences Blank-Adult Form*, 2. The Psychological Corporation.

Spero, M. E. (1987). A Needs Anaysis Survey on the Burnout Phenomenon of Elementary School Teachers.

The CHADD Information and Resource Guide to AD/HD. (2000). Landover, MD: CHADD.

Vitale, B. M. (1982). Unicorns are Real: A Right-Brained Approach to Learning. Rolling Hills Estates, CA: Jalmar Press.

Weschler, D. (2014). Wescher Intelligence Scale for Children-V. *WISC-V*, 19. PsyhCorp. and our Life Experience as Passionate Treating and Evaluating Psychologists...

FLORIDA THE TURTLE WHO THINKS HE'S A DOG
& DR. MITCH SPERO'S
A-D/HD Attention-Deficit/Hyperactivity Disorder
FEELINGS VOCABULARY WORDS GAME!!!

How to Play the Game/Travel Version:

Decide if each Feeling Word is good or bad. For one point, define and describe the Feeling Word. Give an example of when you have felt this way for two points. If you hace selected a word and you do not6 know the meaning of the Feeling Word, another player can give the definition. The player who selected the Feeling Word can still earn one point if he or she can give an example of when they felt that way, or if they feel that way now. Keep score and the first person to earn 25 points wins.

Enjoy the book and the game! Have fun!

By Florida The Turtle & Dr. Mitch

A-D/HD Feelings Vocabulary Words Game
© 2019 Stable Life, L.L.C./ Zonked - 1,000 Feeling Vocabulary Words by 'Dr. Mitch Spero and Florida The Turtle'

1. Abandoned
2. Able
3. Abnormal
4. Absentminded
5. Abused
6. Accepted
7. Accommodated
8. Accomplished
9. Accountable
10. Accused
11. Accurate
12. Acknowledged
13. Active
14. Adaptive
15. Adept
16. Addicted
17. Adequate
18. Adjusted
19. Admired
20. Adorable
21. Adrift
22. Advantaged
23. Adventurous
24. Adversive
25. A-D/HD
26. Affectionate
27. Affirmed
28. Afraid
29. Aggravated
30. Aggressive
31. Agreeable
32. Aimless
33. Alarmed
34. Alert
35. Alienated
36. Alive
37. Alone
38. Aloof
39. Alright
40. Amazed
41. Ambitious
42. Ambivalent
43. Amused
44. Angry
45. Analyzed
46. Animated

47. Anonymous
48. Antagonistic
49. Annoyed
50. Antisocial
51. Anxious
52. Apathetic
53. Apologetic
54. Appalled
55. Appeased
56. Appreciated
57. Apprehensive
58. Approachable
59. Appropriate
60. Argumentative
61. Arrogant
62. Artistic
63. Articulate
64. Ashamed
65. Aspired
66. Assaulted
67. Assertive
68. Assured
69. Athletic
70. Attacked
71. Attractive

72. Authoritative
73. Available
74. Average
75. Avoided
76. Awake
77. Aware
78. Awesome
79. Awful
80. Awkward
81. Babied
82. Babyish
83. Bad
84. Baffled
85. Baited
86. Bashful
87. Beaten
88. Beautiful
89. Believed
90. Belligerent
91. Belittled
92. Berated
93. Best
94. Betrayed
95. Better
96. Bewildered

97. Bigheaded
98. Bitter
99. Blah
100. Blamed
101. Bland
102. Blank
103. Bleak
104. Blue
105. Boisterous
106. Bold
107. Bored
108. Bossed
109. Bossy
110. Bothered
111. Boyish
112. Brainy
113. Bratty
114. Brave
115. Bright
116. Brilliant
117. Broken
118. Bruised
119. Bubbly
120. Bugged
121. Bullied
122. Bummed
123. Bumped
124. Burdened
125. Busy
126. Bypassed
127. Caged
128. Calculating
129. Calloused
130. Calm
131. Candid
132. Capable
133. Captivated
134. Carefree
135. Careful
136. Caring
137. Cautious
138. Celebrated
139. Certain
140. Challenged
141. Changed
142. Changeable
143. Chaotic
144. Charismatic
145. Charming
146. Cheated

147. Cheerful
148. Cherished
149. Childish
150. Chosen
151. Clean
152. Clever
153. Clingy
154. Close
155. Cloudy
156. Clumsy
157. Coached
158. Cold
159. Comfortable
160. Committed
161. Communicative
162. Compassionate
163. Compensated
164. Competitive
165. Competent
166. Complete
167. Completed
168. Complicated
169. Complimented
170. Comprehended
171. Compulsive
172. Concerned
173. Conceited
174. Confident
175. Conflicted
176. Confused
177. Confrontational
178. Congruent
179. Connected
180. Considerate
181. Contempt
182. Contemptuous
183. Content
184. Contradictory
185. Controlled
186. Cool
187. Cooperative
188. Cornered
189. Corrected
190. Courageous
191. Cowardly
192. Cozy
193. Crabby
194. Cranky
195. Creative
196. Critical

197. Criticized
198. Cruel
199. Crummy
200. Cultured
201. Cute
202. Curious
203. Cured
204. Damaged
205. Daring
206. Dark
207. Dazed
208. Deceitful
209. Dedicated
210. Defeated
211. Defective
212. Defensive
213. Defenseless
214. Defiant
215. Deflated
216. Dehumanized
217. Dejected
218. Delayed
219. Delicate
220. Delightful
221. Delusional

222. Demanding
223. Demeaned
224. Demented
225. Demoted
226. Demoralized
227. Denied
228. Dependable
229. Dependent
230. Depleted
231. Depressed
232. Deprived
233. Deserted
234. Deserving
235. Desirable
236. Desired
237. Despaired
238. Desperate
239. Despicable
240. Despised
241. Destructive
242. Detached
243. Determined
244. Detested
245. Devalued
246. Devastated

247. Deviant
248. Devious
249. Different
250. Difficult
251. Direct
252. Directed
253. Dirty
254. Disabled
255. Disadvantaged
256. Disagreeable
257. Disappointed
258. Disciplined
259. Discomforted
260. Disconnected
261. Discouraged
262. Discriminated
263. Disengaged
264. Disgruntled
265. Disgusted
266. Dishonest
267. Disinterested
268. Disjointed
269. Disliked
270. Disobedient
271. Disorganized
272. Displeased
273. Disregarded
274. Disrespected
275. Disrespectful
276. Disruptive
277. Distant
278. Distracted
279. Distraught
280. Distressed
281. Disturbed
282. Dizzy
283. Doubtful
284. Dreamy
285. Driven
286. Drowsy
287. Dull
288. Dutiful
289. Dynamic
290. Dysfunctional
291. Eager
292. Easy
293. Ecstatic
294. Elevated
295. Embarrassed
296. Embraced

297. Emotional
298. Empathetic
299. Empowered
300. Empty
301. Encouraged
302. Endearing
303. Energetic
304. Engaged
305. Engrossed
306. Enjoyment
307. Enlightened
308. Enraged
309. Enriched
310. Entertained
311. Enthusiastic
312. Entitled
313. Envious
314. Equal
315. Esteemed
316. Evil
317. Examined
318. Exasperated
319. Exceptional
320. Excited
321. Excused

322. Exhausted
323. Experienced
324. Exploited
325. Explosive
326. Exposed
327. Extravagant
328. Extreme
329. Extroverted
330. Fabulous
331. Failed
332. Failure
333. Fair
334. Fake
335. Familiar
336. Famous
337. Fanatical
338. Fancy
339. Fantastic
340. Fascinated
341. Fat
342. Faulted
343. Favored
344. Fearful
345. Fearless
346. Festive

347. Fidgety
348. Fiendish
349. Finished
350. Fixated
351. Flabbergasted
352. Flaky
353. Flamboyant
354. Flashy
355. Flat
356. Flattered
357. Flawed
358. Flawless
359. Flexible
360. Flimsy
361. Flirty
362. Focused
363. Followed
364. Foreign
365. Forgetful
366. Forgiving
367. Forgotten
368. Foul
369. Fractured
370. Fragile
371. Frail

372. Frantic
373. Frazzled
374. Freaked
375. Free
376. Fretful
377. Friendly
378. Frightened
379. Frivolous
380. Frustrated
381. Funky
382. Funny
383. Furious
384. Fussy
385. Fuzzy
386. Gallant
387. Garbled
388. Gaudy
389. Geeky
390. Generous
391. Gentle
392. Genuine
393. Ghoulish
394. Giddy
395. Gifted
396. Giggly

397. Girly
398. Giving
399. Glad
400. Gleeful
401. Gloomy
402. Goofy
403. Gorgeous
404. Gossipy
405. Grabby
406. Graceful
407. Gracious
408. Grandiose
409. Grateful
410. Gratified
411. Greedy
412. Grimm
413. Groggy
414. Gross
415. Grouchy
416. Grumpy
417. Guarded
418. Guided
419. Guilty
420. Handicapped
421. Handsome
422. Handy
423. Happy
424. Harassed
425. Hardened
426. Harmed
427. Harmless
428. Harmonious
429. Harsh
430. Hated
431. Hazy
432. Headstrong
433. Healthy
434. Heard
435. Heartbroken
436. Heckled
437. Helped
438. Helpless
439. Heroic
440. Hesitant
441. Hidden
442. Hideous
443. Hilarious
444. Hollow
445. Homesick
446. Honest

447. Honored
448. Hopeful
449. Hopeless
450. Horrified
451. Hostile
452. Humble
453. Humiliated
454. Humorous
455. Hyper
456. Hyperactive
457. Hypersensitive
458. Hyperverbal
459. Hypocritical
460. Idealistic
461. Idiotic
462. Ignored
463. Ill
464. Illogical
465. Impactful
466. Impaired
467. Impartial
468. Impatient
469. Imperfect
470. Impolite
471. Important
472. Imposing
473. Impressed
474. Imprisoned
475. Improved
476. Impulsive
477. Inactive
478. Inadequate
479. Inappropriate
480. Inattentive
481. Incapable
482. Included
483. Incompatible
484. Incompetent
485. Incomplete
486. Inconsolable
487. Incredible
488. Indecisive
489. Independent
490. Indifferent
491. Ineffective
492. Inept
493. Inexperienced
494. Inferior
495. Inflamed
496. Inflicted

497. Inflated
498. Influenced
499. Innocent
500. Insatiable
501. Insecure
502. Insensitive
503. Insignificant
504. Insincere
505. Insistent
506. Inspired
507. Instructed
508. Insufficient
509. Insulted
510. Intellectual
511. Intelligent
512. Interested
513. Interrupted
514. Intimidated
515. Intolerant
516. Intrigued
517. Introverted
518. Intrusive
519. Intuitive
520. Invaluable
521. Inventive
522. Invisible
523. Inviting
524. Irrational
525. Irregular
526. Irrelevant
527. Irreplaceable
528. Irritated
529. Isolated
530. Jazzy
531. Jealous
532. Jilted
533. Jittery
534. Jolly
535. Jostled
536. Jovial
537. Joyful
538. Jubilant
539. Judged
540. Juggled
541. Jumbled
542. Jumpy
543. Junky
544. Justified
545. Just
546. Keen

547. Kind
548. Kindhearted
549. Knowledgeable
550. Labeled
551. Lackadaisical
552. Lacking
553. Ladylike
554. Lagging
555. Lame
556. Large
557. Lavished
558. Lazy
559. Learned
560. Lethargic
561. Liberated
562. Lifeless
563. Liked
564. Limited
565. Limitless
566. Little
567. Lively
568. Livid
569. Loathed
570. Logical
571. Lonely

572. Lonesome
573. Lopsided
574. Lost
575. Lousy
576. Loved
577. Loving
578. Low
579. Loyal
580. Lucid
581. Lucky
582. Lukewarm
583. Mad
584. Magical
585. Malignant
586. Maniacal
587. Manic
588. Manipulated
589. Manipulative
590. Materialistic
591. Mature
592. Mean
593. Meaningful
594. Mechanical
595. Meek
596. Mellow

597. Melodramatic
598. Memorable
599. Merciful
600. Merry
601. Mesmerized
602. Meticulous
603. Miffed
604. Mindless
605. Mischievous
606. Miserable
607. Misguided
608. Mistaken
609. Mistreated
610. Mistrusted
611. Mistrustful
612. Misunderstood
613. Mixed
614. Modest
615. Moody
616. Mortified
617. Motivated
618. Mournful
619. Moved
620. Muddled
621. Mysterious

622. Mystified
623. Nagged
624. Narcissistic
625. Narrowminded
626. Nasty
627. Naughty
628. Nauseated
629. Needed
630. Needy
631. Negative
632. Neglected
633. Nerdy
634. Nervous
635. New
636. Nice
637. Noisy
638. Nosey
639. Nimble
640. Nitpicked
641. Nonessential
642. Nonexistent
643. Normal
644. Nostalgic
645. Nosy
646. Numb

647. Nuts
648. Nutty
649. Obedient
650. Obligated
651. Obnoxious
652. Obscure
653. Observant
654. Observed
655. Obsessed
656. Obsolete
657. Occupied
658. Odd
659. Offended
660. Offensive
661. OK
662. Old
663. Openminded
664. Opposed
665. Oppressed
666. Optimistic
667. Ordinary
668. Organized
669. Ostracized
670. Outcasted
671. Outgoing
672. Outnumbered
673. Outraged
674. Outspoken
675. Outstanding
676. Overanalyzed
677. Overanxious
678. Overbearing
679. Overconfident
680. Overcrowded
681. Overemotional
682. Overestimated
683. Overlooked
684. Overjoyed
685. Overpowered
686. Overruled
687. Overstimulated
688. Overwhelmed
689. Overworked
690. Paced
691. Pained
692. Pampered
693. Panicked
694. Panicky
695. Paranoid
696. Passionate

697. Patient
698. Patronized
699. Peaceful
700. Peachy
701. Peeved
702. Perfect
703. Perplexed
704. Persecuted
705. Persistent
706. Personable
707. Pessimistic
708. Pestered
709. Petrified
710. Petty
711. Pitied
712. Pitiful
713. Plain
714. Playful
715. Pleasant
716. Pleased
717. Polite
718. Pompous
719. Poor
720. Popular
721. Positive
722. Powerful
723. Powerless
724. Preoccupied
725. Preferred
726. Present
727. Pressured
728. Pretty
729. Prickly
730. Prideful
731. Proactive
732. Prioritized
733. Prideful
734. Problematic
735. Protected
736. Protective
737. Proud
738. Provoked
739. Pumped
740. Punished
741. Pushy
742. Puzzled
743. Qualified
744. Quarrelsome
745. Queasy
746. Questioned

747. Quiet
748. Quieted
749. Quirky
750. Quizzed
751. Rational
752. Rattled
753. Rebellious
754. Rebuked
755. Recognized
756. Reckless
757. Regretful
758. Reinforced
759. Rejected
760. Rejuvenated
761. Relaxed
762. Reliable
763. Relieved
764. Reluctant
765. Reliable
766. Remarkable
767. Remembered
768. Resentful
769. Reserved
770. Resilient
771. Resisted
772. Reasonable
773. Resentful
774. Respected
775. Responsible
776. Rested
777. Restless
778. Restricted
779. Revengeful
780. Rewarded
781. Rich
782. Ridiculous
783. Ridiculed
784. Right
785. Righteous
786. Risky
787. Rotten
788. Rude
789. Rushed
790. Ruthless
791. Sacrificed
792. Sad
793. Sadness
794. Safe
795. Satisficed
796. Sarcastic

797. Saved
798. Scared
799. Scrappy
800. Scratched
801. Scrutinized
802. Secretive
803. Secure
804. Sedated
805. Selfish
806. Self-centered
807. Self-destructive
808. Sensitive
809. Sentimental
810. Separated
811. Serious
812. Serene
813. Shaky
814. Shameful
815. Shocked
816. Shy
817. Sick
818. Sickened
819. Sidetracked
820. Significant
821. Silly
822. Sincere
823. Sinister
824. Skeptical
825. Skilled
826. Skinny
827. Skittish
828. Sleepy
829. Sloppy
830. Slow
831. Sluggish
832. Sly
833. Small
834. Smart
835. Sneaky
836. Snobby
837. Social
838. Sophisticated
839. Sore
840. Sorrowful
841. Sorry
842. Special
843. Spectacular
844. Speechless
845. Speedy
846. Spirited

847. Spiteful
848. Splendid
849. Spoiled
850. Spontaneous
851. Spooked
852. Spunky
853. Squeamish
854. Stable
855. Startled
856. Strange
857. Stressed
858. Stimulated
859. Strong
860. Stubborn
861. Studious
862. Stunned
863. Stupendous
864. Stupid
865. Stylish
866. Successful
867. Suffocated
868. Sulky
869. Supervised
870. Supported
871. Surpassed

872. Surprised
873. Suspicious
874. Swamped
875. Sweet
876. Sympathetic
877. Tactful
878. Tactless
879. Talented
880. Talkative
881. Taunted
882. Tearful
883. Teased
884. Tempted
885. Terrible
886. Terrified
887. Tested
888. Thankful
889. Thoughtful
890. Thoughtless
891. Threatened
892. Thrifty
893. Thrilled
894. Tidy
895. Timid
896. Tiny

897. Tired
898. Tolerated
899. Tormented
900. Tough
901. Trapped
902. Triumphant
903. Troubled
904. Trusted
905. Trusting
906. Trustworthy
907. Ugly
908. Unable
909. Unaccepted
910. Unappreciated
911. Uncertain
912. Uncomfortable
913. Unconnected
914. Uncooperative
915. Undecided
916. Understood
917. Underestimated
918. Underrated
919. Uneasy
920. Unexceptional
921. Unfriendly

922. Unfortunate
923. Unhappy
924. Unhealthy
925. Unimportant
926. Unintelligent
927. United
928. Unlikeable
929. Unlovable
930. Unloved
931. Unlucky
932. Unmotivated
933. Unpleasant
934. Unprepared
935. Unqualified
936. Unreasonable
937. Unresolved
938. Unsafe
939. Unsatisfied
940. Unselfish
941. Unsure
942. Unsympathetic
943. Unusual
944. Unwilling
945. Unwelcome
946. Unworthy

947. Upright
948. Upset
949. Used
950. Useful
951. Useless
952. Validated
953. Valued
954. Vengeful
955. Victimized
956. Victorious
957. Violated
958. Vindictive
959. Violent
960. Virtuous
961. Vulnerable
962. Wacky
963. Wanted
964. Warned
965. Warmhearted
966. Wary
967. Wasteful
968. Watched
969. Weak
970. Wealthy
971. Weary

972. Wealthy
973. Weird
974. Welcome
975. Wholesome
976. Whipped
977. Wicked
978. Wiggly
979. Wild
980. Willing
981. Wimpy
982. Wise
983. Wishful
984. Withdrawn
985. Witty
986. Whiney
987. Wonderful
988. Worried
989. Worthless
990. Worthy
991. Wounded
992. Wronged
993. Young
994. Youthful
995. Yucky
996. Zainey

997. Zapped

998. Zealous

999. Zippy

1000. Zonked

Create your own
feeling word.
I feel "_____."

Create your own
feeling word.
I feel "_____."

Create your own
feeling word.
I feel "_____."

Create your own
feeling word.
I feel "_____."

Create your own
feeling word.
I feel "_____."

Create your own
feeling word.
I feel "_____."

www.ingramcontent.com/pod-product-compliance
Lightning Source LLC
Chambersburg PA
CBHW051224120626
46547CB00013B/1500

9 798889 391641 6